UNLEASHING POTENTIAL

confidence

30 Messages in **30** Days to empower you
to be a better, more confident you!

JUSTIN PATTON

UNLEASHING POTENTIAL: Confidence
by Justin Patton

Limit of Liability/Disclaimer of Warranty:
While the author has used his best efforts in preparing this book, he makes no representations or warranties with respect to the accuracy or completeness of the contents of this book and specifically disclaim any implied warranties of merchantability or fitness for a particular purpose. The advice and strategies contained here may not be suitable for your situation. You should consult with a professional where appropriate. The author shall not be liable for any loss of profit or any other commercial damages, including but not limited to special, incidental, consequential, or other damages.

UNLEASHING POTENTIAL: Confidence
30 Messages in 30 Days to empower you to be a better, more confident you!

ISBN 978-1-7328766-2-0 (paperback)

Written by Justin Patton
Photography by Chad Bock
Cover design, typography and layout by Shaina Nielson

DEDICATION

This book is written for every person who hasn't felt good enough and had to grow up without the self-love and mental toughness they needed.

I honor your journey,
and I hope this book
helps **unleash in you**
the unshakable *courage*
and *confidence* you desire.

There is nothing more important in this world than your belief in yourself.

What you believe, or don't believe, about yourself becomes the filter for how you show up in the world, how you make decisions, and how you treat yourself and others.

Confidence is having the courage to show up as yourself and for yourself – even when that choice feels risky, uncomfortable, or even scary. Confidence does not require you to have it all together or to be the loudest person in the room. It does, however, require you to master a deep level of self-awareness and self-acceptance of both your strengths and weaknesses.

When we have not developed this strong sense of self-awareness and self-acceptance then our confidence becomes situational – like a light-switch that we have no control over. Our confidence is switched "on" when we find ourselves in moments where we are comfortable, but the moment we step into something new, something uncomfortable the switch goes "off," the negative stories start racing through our mind, and we walk into every room feeling our identity is on the line. As a result, we never show up our best because we're trying to sell people on why they should buy into us and we don't take risks that could put us in the place of most potential.

I look back on my life and I can pinpoint multiple situations where my confidence was eroded because I put more weight in what other people thought about me rather than what I thought about myself. This caused me to think, *Am I good enough?* This single, and often unconscious, thought does the most damage to our belief in ourselves.

When I didn't feel good enough, I wouldn't speak up. I became judgmental of others, and I would blame other people for robbing me of my joy. Then I woke up one day and realized I was the one robbing myself. I had made myself a victim and given every bit of my personal power to other people. And with that realization, I took it back!

I made some difficult choices to re-experience life with new vision, with new boundaries, and with a newfound sense of confidence. I stopped allowing other people's opinions and situations to dictate my belief in myself. I stopped believing the ridiculous notion that I had to have it all together. I stopped being the person I thought people wanted me to be, and I honored the truth of who I was - and had always been. I stopped being afraid to speak up and share my voice. I stopped believing the negative thoughts I had said about myself for years. As a result, everything in my life changed. More importantly, I slowly started learning how to unconditionally love the person I was - regardless of whether that made other people proud, disappointed, or uncomfortable.

Authentic confidence comes from being able to wake up every morning and radically love the person staring back at you in the mirror.

Confidence is about putting the need to like yourself over the need to be liked by others. It is not being egocentric without any care of what other people think. Confident people do care about others and they value what others think. They do not, however, wear those thoughts and feedback on their soul as signs of their worthiness. Having confidence does not mean that you are never uncomfortable or fearful. It means you have the willingness to show up anyways and not allow those emotions to hold you back from the truth of who you are.

I do not know what has transpired in your life, what you are currently going through, or what you see when you look in the mirror. What I do know, however, is that if you want to maximize your potential, engage in healthy relationships, and be the leader you are meant to be then you must develop authentic confidence.

My experience speaking to thousands of people a year and coaching leaders in Fortune 500 organizations, NCAA athletes, and contestants in the Miss America and Miss USA pageants has taught me one fundamental lesson: **external success does not equate to confidence!**

I have worked with NCAA athletes who had a track record of winning in their sport but felt lost and defeated after being injured and unable to play. I have coached contestants in the Miss America pageant system who won a myriad number of crowns and titles, but who could not articulate who they are or stand resolute in articulating their views. I have coached leaders who made it to the top of their field but struggled developing mutually beneficial relationships in their life. They did not let people see their true self because they were not even comfortable with that version of themselves. Other leaders were dragging a lifetime of hurt and unreconciled baggage behind them. They coped by throwing themselves into their career and using their job to validate their self-worth. Other leaders talked a big game and exuded bravado in how they communicate with others. Their armor and tough exterior were just a defense to what they actually felt inside.

If you picked up this book then you are like many others who know they are capable of playing bigger but need to work on developing their confidence so it shows up in their actions. The most authentically confident people are the most self-aware people. Therefore, this book is going to empower you to become more self-aware about who you are, cultivate stronger emotional intelligence, and take intentional action to move forward in your life.

WHAT YOU SHOULD KNOW ABOUT CONFIDENCE

When becoming certified in emotional intelligence, I learned that self-regard is one of the biggest influencers to how we view ourselves, how we communicate and build relationships, how we make decisions, and how we handle stress in our lives.

Confidence is a mindset, and it does not require you to prove it to anyone else. Additionally, confidence is not a fixed trait. We know that it can be cultivated and developed throughout life. Where you are and how you see yourself today does not have to dictate where you want to be in the future.

Just 15 minutes of intentional daily reflection, for the next 30 days, can help you cultivate stronger confidence and develop the mental toughness you need to be successful and happy.

This book is going to create the space you need to. . .

1. Build a stronger relationship with yourself
2. Address negative self-talk and limiting beliefs
3. Reframe your past experiences
4. Set boundaries that serve and honor who you are
5. Create a vision for your future
6. Decide on and take intentional action

HOW TO GET THE MOST OUT OF THIS BOOK

1. Read each haiku twice. On the second reading, read it slow and put emphasis on the words that resonate with you.

2. Spend 5-15 minutes each day reflecting on the empowering questions on the adjacent page. Reflect in a way that best supports your style and growth. Some of you may choose to write your reflection in the space provided so you have a journal that you can keep. Some of you may want to reflect in the shower or in your car, and others of you may want to reflect by having a conversation about the questions with your friend, partner, co-workers. It doesn't matter how you reflect, as long as you do!

3. Commit to taking a minimum of one specific action based on your daily reflection.

4. Check-in with yourself after 7 messages by completing the weekly reflection.

One of the most fundamental steps in developing your authentic confidence is having the boldness to invest in yourself. You have made a decision to show up for yourself. I am proud of you and I am honored to be a part of your journey.

Continue to show up for yourself and go after everything your heart desires. It is waiting for you!

LET'S GET STARTED!!!

UNLEASHING POTENTIAL

Sometimes you will want
Permission to PLAY **bigger.**
Permission granted!

Reflection Questions

1. How would showing up with more confidence impact your career and relationships?
2. If you could write yourself a permission slip with all the things you need to give yourself permission to do, what would be on your permission slip?

My Commitment

What is one action you will take today based on your reflection?

INSIDE OF YOU IS Someone *fearless* and brave so Let that *person* **SHINE.**

Reflection Questions

1. List all the actions confident people demonstrate.
2. When have you demonstrated those traits in the past?

My Commitment

What is one action you will take today based on your reflection?

Reflection Questions

1. What thoughts do you sometimes tell yourself that make you feel like you are not good enough?
2. Who would you be without those thoughts?

My Commitment

What is one action you will take today based on your reflection?

Reflection Questions

1. List 5–10 actions you would take if you put yourself first.
2. What would be the benefits, to you and others, of following through on some of the ideas you listed?

My Commitment

What is one action you will take today based on your reflection?

Reflection Questions

1. Confident people take risks and sometimes fail, so what is another way to look at failure so it serves you and the goals you want to achieve as you move forward?
2. How have some of your short-term "failures" helped you be successful long-term?

My Commitment

What is one action you will take today based on your reflection?

Reflection Questions

1. What unnecessary limits have you put on yourself in the past?
2. How have those limits held you back?

My Commitment

What is one action you will take today based on your reflection?

You might feel **stuck** but
Your choices **lead to freedom.**
make another *choice!*

Reflection Questions

1. What area of your life do you currently feel stuck?
2. What is the single, most important choice you could make that would start to move you in the direction you want to go?

My Commitment

What is one action you will take today based on your reflection?

WEEKLY REFLECTION

What did you learn about yourself over the past week?

What are 5 things you are *grateful* for during the past week?

On a scale of 1–10 (with 1 being "very little" and 10 being "an extraordinary amount"), how much did you grow your confidence this past week? Explain your answer.

What is your *intention* for next week?

A CHAMPION IS A person who **RISES UP** – *again and again…*

Reflection Questions

1. What specific actions do champions demonstrate?
2. When have you demonstrated those attributes?

My Commitment

What is one action you will take today based on your reflection?

SPEAK UP. *Own* **your voice.**
What you have to say *matters.*
SILENCE IS A CHOICE.

Reflection Questions

1. How would you use your voice differently if you could believe that people needed to hear your message in only the way you can say it?
2. In what situations do you need to speak up and be more assertive?

My Commitment

What is one action you will take today based on your reflection?

I FOUND *a new me* WHEN I STARTED TO **ENJOY** *my own company.*

Reflection Questions

1. What are 5 activities (regardless of how well you do them) that bring you joy and re-energize you?
2. How can you cultivate more of those activities into your life?

My Commitment

What is one action you will take today based on your reflection?

Reflection Questions

1. What is a goal you have been putting off that want to accomplish?
2. Imagine you have achieved that goal. What advice would you look back and tell yourself now from that point-of-view?

My Commitment

What is one action you will take today based on your reflection?

Reflection Questions

1. How would you feel if you could believe it was going to get better in time?
2. What step(s) do you need to take so you can heal yourself?

My Commitment

What is one action you will take today based on your reflection?

I AM NOT MY PAST.
Join me right where I am *now*
Or kindly leave me.

Reflection Questions

1. How have you changed from the person you used to be?
2. What relationships do you need to re-negotiate in life?

My Commitment

What is one action you will take today based on your reflection?

If no one tells you
THEY **believe in you** TODAY,
I believe in you!

Reflection Questions

1. What insight and encouragement did your younger self need to hear?
2. How can that insight and encouragement help you now?

My Commitment

What is one action you will take today based on your reflection?

WEEKLY REFLECTION

CONFIDENCE

What did you learn about yourself over the past week?

What are 5 things you are *grateful* for during the past week?

On a scale of 1–10 (with 1 being "very little" and 10 being "an extraordinary amount"), how much did you grow your confidence this past week? Explain your answer.

What is your *intention* for next week?

THERE IS *no mistake*
WHERE YOU ARE IN YOUR JOURNEY:
YOU ARE **UNFINISHED...**

Reflection Questions

1. Explain what being "unfinished" means to you?
2. How can you use that definition to motivate yourself moving forward?

My Commitment

What is one action you will take today based on your reflection?

Reflection Questions

1. What are your strengths and natural talents?
2. List a minimum of 3 things you admire about yourself.

My Commitment

What is one action you will take today based on your reflection?

SPEND YOUR TIME WITH THOSE
WHO MAKE YOU A **BETTER YOU.**
YOU *won't* REGRET IT.

Reflection Questions

1. List 5–10 people (personally and professionally) you trust and value.
2. How do you show your appreciation to them?

My Commitment

What is one action you will take today based on your reflection?

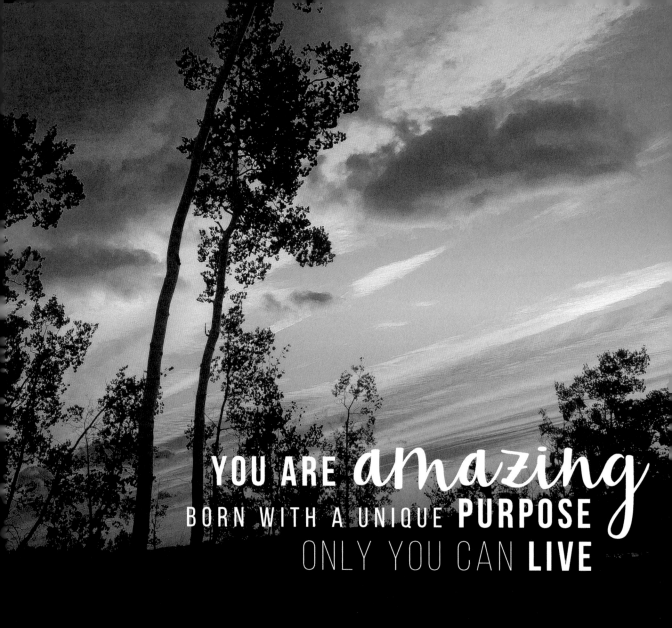

YOU ARE *amazing*
BORN WITH A UNIQUE **PURPOSE**
ONLY YOU CAN **LIVE**

Reflection Questions

1. How do you define purpose?
2. How has your past shaped your purpose in life?

My Commitment

What is one action you will take today based on your reflection?

Reflection Questions

1. What changes do you need to make so you fully accept your authentic self?
2. What do you need to forgive yourself or others for?

My Commitment

What is one action you will take today based on your reflection?

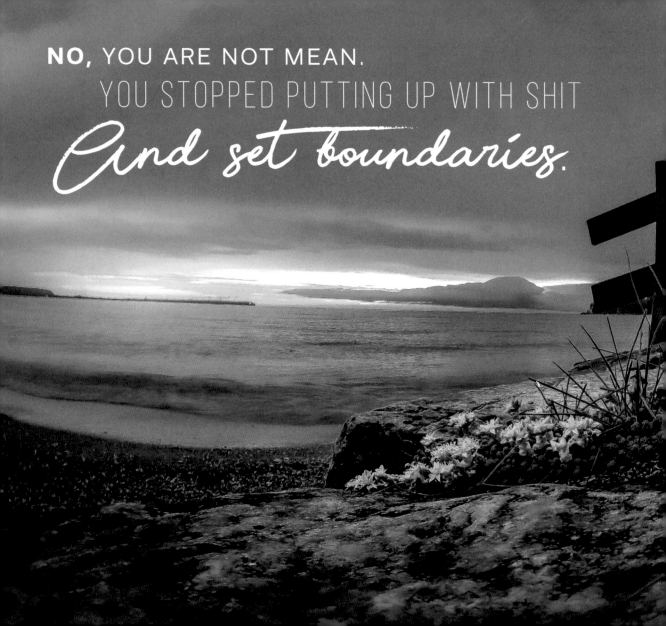

Reflection Questions

1. What are your core four boundaries that must be present in all relationships in your life (i.e. trust, transparent communication, growth, spirituality) so that you can show up your best?
2. What happens when they are not present?

My Commitment

What is one action you will take today based on your reflection?

You are never stuck. You are just **one choice away** from a *bold new you!*

Reflection Questions

1. What is the "next right choice" for you...
2. Emotionally? Spirituality? Socially? Intellectually? Financially? Physically?

My Commitment

What is one action you will take today based on your reflection?

WEEKLY REFLECTION

What did you learn about yourself over the past week?

What are 5 things you are *grateful* for during the past week?

On a scale of 1–10 (with 1 being "very little" and 10 being "an extraordinary amount"), how much did you grow your confidence this past week? Explain your answer.

What is your *intention* for next week?

You are free to live
A life *bigger* and *bolder*
THAN WHERE YOU ARE NOW.

Reflection Questions

1. What does a bigger and bolder life look like for you?
2. Who can you share that vision with so they can support you?

My Commitment

What is one action you will take today based on your reflection?

Don't be afraid to

ASK FOR HELP when *you need it.*

DON'T DROWN QUIETLY.

Reflection Questions

1. What are some things you need to ask for help on right now?
2. What has held you back from asking for help when you needed it?

My Commitment

What is one action you will take today based on your reflection?

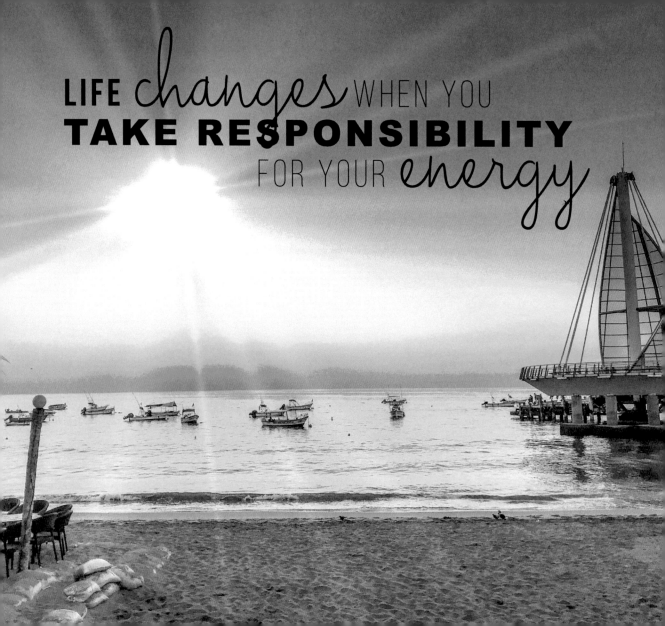

Reflection Questions

1. How do you want to be perceived by others?
2. How are the presence and mindset you show up with most often getting you what you want or holding you back?

My Commitment

What is one action you will take today based on your reflection?

STOP AND **INTRODUCE** YOURSELF TO THE PERSON YOU *aspire to be.*

Reflection Questions

1. Who would you be if you had the confidence you wanted?
2. What will it take to be that person?

My Commitment

What is one action you will take today based on your reflection?

SOMETIMES LIFE IS **HARD**

UNEXPECTED THINGS HAPPEN

Reflection Questions

1. Recall a time you had to overcome a difficult situation in your life. What specific steps did you take to overcome the situation?
2. How can you leverage those steps in the future?

My Commitment

What is one action you will take today based on your reflection?

DO NOT BE AFRAID
To walk into the spotlight.
you are meant to shine.

Reflection Questions

1. If you were going to walk into the spotlight and be known for something, what would you want to be known for?
2. In what area(s) do you want to develop your competence so you can achieve that vision?

My Commitment

What is one action you will take today based on your reflection?

YOU WILL NEVER BE
fully ready for **what's next.**
Do it anyway!

Reflection Questions

1. What are some actions you would start doing if you could release yourself from the idea that you had to be 100% ready before starting?
2. What one bold step would the confident you take right now?

My Commitment

What is one action you will take today based on your reflection?

You are the author
Of a story worth telling.
Share it with the world!

Reflection Questions

1. If you could offer one piece of advice to others, based on your journey, what would it be and why?
2. How has your past shaped the value you bring into every situation?

My Commitment

What is one action you will take today based on your reflection?

Reflection Questions

1. What "mantra" would your courageous self tell you when you get scared or reluctant?
2. How can you use this mantra moving forward to empower you?

My Commitment

What is one action you will take today based on your reflection?

FINAL REFLECTION

"*THERE IS NOTHING* **MORE IMPORTANT** *THAN YOUR* **BELIEF IN** *yourself*"

My unique *strengths* are...

The *mantra* my confident self will live by is...

Actions I exhibit when I am confident are...

receptive and inviting to such activation. These experiences are extremely pleasurable if entered into with an openness to new sensations. This can be experienced by the ecstatic movement in rhythm that flows through the individual when moving to music, such as at a festival.

Following are a few of the leading festivals in the United States:

1. Bonnaroo Music and Arts Festival in Manchester, Tennessee
2. Traverse City Film Festival in Michigan, founded by Michael Moore
3. Aspen Music Festival in Aspen, Colorado
4. Burning Man in Black Rock Desert, Nevada
5. Williamstown Theater Festival in Williamstown, Massachusetts
6. Artscape in Baltimore, Maryland
7. Jacob's Pillow Dance Festival in Western Massachusetts

There are cellular and molecular processes that are being activated by these rushes of energy and motion. Together they make emotion, and they can serve as the building blocks for a new worldview that understands the vital role that the ecstatic mystical experience has played in human evolution. It is its purpose. There are large groups of people going through these activities at ongoing music and self-expression festivals. This is happening now, and we should welcome this behind-the-scenes process.

The ability to understand what is happening here on earth is a rare trait among humans. This guide is meant to assist in the expanding of humanity's horizons and the opening of hearts and minds.

Rock and roll and other types of music are particularly valuable tools to help one undergo and understand the activation processes. This is because of the effect that music has on the listener, both in a mood alteration and an inspirational sense. Perhaps the greatest role that music can play is to get people moving in harmony and synchronicity. Music can also carry a message, as John Lennon, Jim Morrison, and others have shown us.

The fiftieth anniversary of the Woodstock festival came this past summer. That event showed all society that a cultural movement has been spreading and growing through the land for the past fifty years. The counterculture of the 1960s and 1970s has reached late middle age, and it is about to emerge fully formed onto the scene. It is a positive vibration of peace, love, and cooperation. It is this spirit that will sweep over the nation and the planet and get us past this era of oppression and domination.

In our society, rock and roll is a primary means by which people go through the activation process. This is largely because corporations have taken over rock music and now stage large for-profit concerts. These are helpful, but the more meaningful forms of music involve participation by more of the people present, such as sing-alongs and drumming circles. These allow the individuals to be a part of the creative process and thereby find the flow for themselves. This is difficult logistically in our society, but people must persist in discovering their inner creativity.

People need to realize the stakes that we are playing with. We are the generation that will determine whether there is a future for humanity here on earth. We are in uncharted territory.

Raising the Level of Consciousness

These processes lead to an ever-increasing level of awareness or consciousness. This process must be cultivated and worked with if it is to bear sweet fruit, but that is the challenge of the person who wishes to experience the ecstatic joy and rapture of the flow or movement from the Source. It is a torrent of energy that makes one feel alive, awakened, and eventually enlightened. The task is for as many people as possible to undergo this process under the guidance of experienced seekers so that the level of oneness and joy can be elevated in time to lift humanity to a higher level of consciousness.

Wikipedia describes religious ecstasy as "the type of altered state of consciousness characterized by greatly reduced external awareness and expanded interior and mental and spiritual awareness, frequently accompanied by visions and emotional and sometimes physical euphoria."[1] The ecstatic experience is at the heart of all true spirituality. It can be accessed through meditation, exercise, yoga, tantric sex, drumming, music, dance, and use of the shamanic plants. This is the type of experience that must be encouraged and facilitated if we are to get through the shakes and quakes to the jewel in the wake. This will result in the earth emerging as a shimmering jewel in the wake of an awakened and enlightened humanity. It is in this way that we were

---

[1] "Religious ecstasy," Wikipedia, last updated September 17, 2019, https://en.wikipedia.org/wiki/Religious_ecstasy.

conceived and came into the world, and it is in this way that the new world will be conceived and born.

As this new understanding and consciousness spreads, people will begin coming together to celebrate victory over the ignorance and lies that have prevented humanity from seeing the truth and reconnecting to the Source. This will lead to the awakening happenings that will sprout up all over the countryside in anticipation of the larger, global celebration to commemorate the new golden age as well as the end of war in a "thought creates reality" sort of way.

Once awakened, each individual must be prepared to be held to account if he or she was unable to help steer humanity toward a safer course. We are held to account by our higher selves and our Creator. Many star seeds came here for this purpose, and failing to discover and act on that would be very unfortunate. This need only be accomplished on the thought level, however, because thought creates reality. The seeker is to be reassured that there are spirit guides ready and willing to help humans with their quest for spiritual enlightenment and ultimate truth.

The change agent then needs to recognize the sign of activation and to connect with the insights and synchronicities that may be occurring in his or her life. This includes the conscious surrender of will to the Source in all its facets, combined with a steely resolve that the world foundation will be saved, whatever it takes.

The actual physiological activation process (PAP) involves imbibing and partaking of certain substances and participating in as many forbidden and forgotten rituals as one is able. This includes many types of psychoactive plants. Those employed throughout human history include cannabis, coca, opium, morphine, khat, mescaline, peyote, psilocybin, mushrooms, and DMT, according to Wikipedia. Also, spontaneous and structured movement of all types can assist in this process, as can more sensual forms of release. This process is not well understood in modern industrial nations, but it has been understood by countless generations of indigenous peoples across the globe, as well as by restless youth the world over for the latter half of the past century.

This process is pivotal for people to activate their own truth detectors and gain the ability to see, feel, and experience the oneness and bliss that comes from the transcendent mystical experience. This experience is one of joy and oneness with all, and it involves a sense of being truly alive that is rarely experienced by those who are not seeking. Undergoing the PAP process involves conscious intent. It doesn't necessarily need to be communicated verbally, but there needs to be some awareness that the process is ongoing and under way. The key to the PAP is that it must be sought out and undertaken in order to be appreciated, but it can sneak up on one when one is least expecting it, and those can be the most glorious moments of all.

A good way of integrating music with movement is to listen to various types of music and practice moving rhythmically or flowing with the music. This helps the activation process by opening the energy channels that run throughout the body. These channels can get blocked or may not be properly activated if one is ignorant or unaware of the activation process. You can actually feel the flow or movement from the Source moving through your body if this music and movement combination is done with any regularity. Most people have some familiarity with the activation process. They just think of it as having fun or partying.

There is a strong case to be made for the mushroom spore as an evolutionary driver that, along with other psychedelic plants, has assisted humanity through its long journey here on earth. panspermia theory poses that life came to Earth from another place, according to Will Wright of NPR. It has also been argued that alien civilizations have used spores to spread these consciousness-raising agents here on this planet. It is clear that we need all the help we can get.

Nothing New

This correspondence is being given to all who wish to have a better understanding of the changes that are currently happening in the world. Specifically, we are referring to a dimension shift that will drastically alter reality as it is perceived and experienced. A new paradigm is emerging, and the old ways are falling away. Cooperation, love, and peaceful coexistence will be the hallmarks of the new consciousness here on earth.

This new reality is resulting and will result from a great acceleration in the speed of electrons, a quickening of the molecules in human bodies as well as a dramatic acceleration in the rate of technological development in the greater society. According to the prophecies of the ancient Maya, Hopi, and Egyptians, and peoples of other prominent cultures, the time has come for the end of the old age and the beginning of something totally new.

The most significant thing that we earth humans can do is to anchor in the higher frequencies that will continue to accelerate as history nears its climax over the next few years. The time of the most rapid changes, 2012–2022, is the cusp period at the end of the great cycle of nearly twenty-six thousand years, which is broken up into twelve astrological ages, each of about two thousand years in duration.

This entering into the age of Aquarius is an entering into an air sign, which means increased mental telepathy, astral travel, and access to higher levels of intelligence and understanding. The shift may be accompanied by some turbulence in the atmosphere. This is seen by many as being a necessary part of the transformation, the earth's purification of itself. This could be manifest by extremes in weather conditions and storms, overall climatological changes, or perhaps even a shift in the earth's poles.

People must work together to resolve these problems collectively, just as people must spend time alone to get in touch with their inner and higher selves. The Source says to be aware of the changes that are going on in the world, and don't be afraid to get involved if you see a spot where you feel you can help shift the course of human evolution toward the ways of the Source.

Sports and the Source

The impact of the flow techniques on athletic performance should not be dismissed. This outpouring of the flow from spirit can be seen when an athlete is in the zone, seemingly able to do no wrong and appearing to have activated near superhuman abilities. In athletics, and particularly in tennis, as one climbs the proverbial and literal ladder, one relies more on instinct and muscle reactions and less on conscious thought. More importantly, athletic pursuits of all types, particularly those that have a movement or dance aspect, can be effective tools for undergoing the PAP, if one understands the process. The sport that I would most recommend as a means of activating the PAP is tennis. I make this suggestion because of the mind–body connection inherent in the sport, along with the individual and never-ending qualities of the game. Tennis requires a unique combination of mental and physical abilities. Whatever the level of play, any activity that requires the body and mind to work together seamlessly has to have a positive effect on the individual. Life is a melding of mind and body, and tennis allows that to happen.

The connection to both athletics and the wisdom of the indigenous peoples of earth shows the longevity and adaptability of the PAP. In sports, it can best be understood as the feeling that flows through someone when performing at his or her peak, when body, mind, and spirit are functioning in perfect harmony and the athlete is able to raise his or her level of performance to previously unimagined heights. This is commonly referred to as "being in the zone."

Athletics offer us an excellent way to understand the mind–body connection, teach us how we can learn from past successes and failures, and show us how we can get to know ourselves and our world better. This should be encouraged in people who are willing. They are often considered pure competition, but there should be a greater emphasis on the creative and artistic aspects of sport. This should lead to more female participation, as sports are a valuable tool to teach males about grace and beauty.

In ancient cultures, the PAP was best understood as the result of ecstatic dance and ritual in celebration of the various gods and goddesses of their respective traditions. The PAP was often enhanced by various sacramental elements such as rhythmic drumming, chanting, body piercing, and the sacramental use of shamanic plants. The PAP experience has also been described in relation to the native hunt, as well as the vision quest and other initiatory rituals.

Encyclopedia Britannica says a vision quest is "a supernatural experience in which an individual seeks to interact with a guardian spirit to obtain advice or protection."[2] A vision quest is often considered a ritual marking the individual's transition from childhood to adulthood.

Sports can help fulfill this role if the participant is sufficiently aware to realize how athletic movement can be used to further the activation process. Unfortunately, our ultracompetitive culture makes it rare for a young athlete to be able to take advantage of the athletic field to further his or her spiritual consciousness, but the exercise alone helps one to get the energy moving throughout the body and clears the passageways for the next step, spiritual activation.

---

[2] Encyclopedia Britannica, "Vision quest" accessed 1/14, 2020, https://EncyclopiaBrittanica.com/vision quest

The Spiritual Consciousness Activation Process

igher levels of consciousness are the purpose and plan of the God/Goddess, the Prime Creator, the Source of all that is. We must be bold and daring in seeking to access these higher levels of consciousness. There are always risks involved in life, but the rewards of making breakthroughs in the field of consciousness expansion far outweigh any personal difficulties that the seeker may encounter in said pursuit. These include cosmic enlightenment and the activation of one's own, personal truth detector, as well as activation of the pineal gland, a.k.a. the third eye.

The pineal gland is a pine cone shaped gland that is located in the brain and helps humans see and experience aspects of life that are undetectable with the five senses. It is hidden in plain sight in structures throughout the world as ancient peoples were far more aware of its value and usefulness than people are today. René Descartes believed the human pineal gland to be the "principal seat of the soul."

Meditation is a key part of the spiritual consciousness activation process (SCAP). This comes down to awareness of awareness. There are many types of meditation, and they can be broken down into two categories, stationary and mobile. This process involves letting your thoughts pass by, noticing them but not engaging with them. It is a passive process. Meditation gives the observer a more evolved perspective. This is an important step in gaining a larger perspective on the human experience.

It must be understood that the activity that the fearmongers and paranoid dinosaurs of the old world most fear is that we have a massive movement of people willing to undergo both the PAP and the SCAP. Once these processes are under way within the individual, they play a pivotal role in raising the level of consciousness here on earth and thereby do their part to save the world foundation and sweep aside the old ways of the dark side.

Hence both the physiological and spiritual consciousness activation processes have significant political implications as both can help the individual reconnect to the Source of all that is and hence see through the lies and distortions that have masqueraded as truth for the past half century. The seeker, in most cases, will not get permission from either parents or society to initiate these processes, but it is imperative that they be understood and undertaken by as many people as possible during the early 2020s as this is our best hope for having a smooth and harmonious global transformation.

The importance of going through both the PAP and the SCAP cannot be overstated as these are the keys to experiencing the flow or movement from the Source for oneself and to understanding what one is experiencing. Reconnecting with the Source does take some effort on the part of the searcher. It requires an open mind and a sense of curiosity and wonder. It requires a willingness to follow a line of thought or insight to its conclusion and the ability to put together seemingly unrelated bits of information and stimuli to arrive at a glimpse of the truth.

Spiritual consciousness requires an open mind and an open heart. We learn and grow best when we are accepting of new information, insights, feelings, and understandings. One way to understand the process one takes to ascend is: LAST, TIP, SEE, LAY, EGO, BE. This is an acronym that means Love, Allow, Surrender to the Source, Trust in the Universe. Trust in the Process, Simply Enjoy Everything, Laugh at yourself. Emerging Galactic Organism, Be Enlightened & Be Extraordinary. The process is one of letting go, releasing, and surrendering to the flow or Movement from the Source.

How to Activate

The physiological aspects of the transformation can be accessed through sports, music, dance, drumming, yoga, meditation, or psychoactive plants. One tip is that psychoactive plants can be used in concert with any of the other methods to accelerate the activation process. The spiritual component consists of consciously opening a channel for higher intelligence to flow through and activate both the pleasure and knowing centers, which are closely related. Higher intelligence permeates the galaxy. It is the creative impulse that moves evolution forward.

This process involves some reading and exposure to whichever spiritual traditions most interest and appeal to the individual. This is important because the Movement from the Source and the new spirituality both borrow heavily from historic spiritual traditions that go back thousands of years. Hence any profound understanding of spiritual consciousness requires the seeker to undergo a study of several types of spiritual traditions and use them as the backdrop from which to construct his or her personal pantheon.

Fortunately, there is more information on spirituality and on the many diverse traditions believed and practiced on this planet than there has ever been in history. Furthermore, the link between the new spiritual and scientific breakthroughs in genetics, quantum physics, chaos theory, and the morphogenic field point the way to a new understanding of the true nature of ourselves and of reality. Rupert Sheldrake's morphic field theory and morphic resonance, conveying a collective instinctive memory, sent shock waves through both the scientific and religious communities.

The task of the neophyte spiritual initiate is to become familiar with a diverse cross section of spiritual beliefs and traditions and then to pick and choose those aspects that resonate with his or her core being. This is facilitated by using the PAP to access the quicker, less dense vibrational frequencies that are associated with the SCAP. These frequencies are associated with the fifth, sixth, and seventh chakras, and the third eye and crown chakras, the latter being the center for telepathy and oneness with cosmic consciousness.

Katherine Hurst writes that there are seven basic chakras, or wheels, that start at the top of the head and end at the base of the spine. The idea of chakras traces back to early Hinduism and Buddhism, which stress the importance of keeping them open and aligned.

The seven chakras are as follows:

1. The root or tailbone chakra
2. The sacral or abdomen chakra
3. The solar plexus or stomach chakra
4. The heart chakra
5. The throat chakra
6. The third eye or brow chakra
7. The crown or head chakra.

Dictionary.com defines telepathy as, "the supposed communication of thoughts or ideas by means other than the known senses. Telepathy will become a primary means of communication in the future.

It is time for humanity's next big step, namely, to contact and interact with beings from throughout the galaxy and to join with the Galactic Federation. This is humanity's coming-out party, the end of the quarantine. There is a catch, however. Extreme militarism and weapons of mass destruction are not permitted for use by members of the Galactic Federation. We must come together and renounce war if we are to make the next great leap for humankind.

The most important thing required for the activation process is for the initiate to want to undergo the process. This requires conscious intent, an element that is sorely missing from the flurry of physical activity that one sees all around. This means that one should be aware that one is undergoing a spiritual activation process as one goes about one's day, and particularly when one is in motion as all movement flows from the Source in one form or another. This can be understood as a moving meditation.

Meditation is a relatively easy and basically free way to begin the spiritual consciousness activation process. All it requires is for one to be still, to calm the mind, and to observe the thoughts that flow through the mind. Meditation is a good place to start for one who is seeking a stronger connection with spirit. As one progresses, life can become an active meditation where the seeker gets real-time feedback and inspiration from the world around him or her.

Consciousness Is Awareness of Awareness

It should be understood by the seeker that every activity holds the seed of the activation process, if one is open to and aware of the flow of spirit, which tends to find those who seek it out. It all comes down to listening to your body, trusting your instincts, and knowing that we are here for a grand purpose. Once humanity's divine heritage is understood, these activation processes will be an accepted part of everyone's daily life. Until that time, it is up to the few fearless voyagers who are willing to lead the way through the millennium period into the age of Aquarius.

Higher consciousness is an important but hard to reach mental state. We spend most of our lives in lower levels of consciousness, using the reptilian brain. Accessing higher consciousness requires that one constantly be looking behind the veil for the peak experience, that glimpse beyond ordinary reality to the behind-the-scenes workings of those forces that really make things happen. Like everything else, this applies on several levels, but the SCAP requires one to constantly be searching for the voice behind the voice, for the questions behind the answers. We must continually peel away the levels of lies, illusion, and distortion so we can once again be connected to the bright light of truth and knowing that flows from the Source of all that is.

We give meaning to life, both individually and collectively. The highest purpose of life is to help others. The meaning for this generation is to help humanity get through the present challenges and join with the galactic community. This is the time for action, for bold plans to bring about stability and sustainability. One must be willing to accept some degree of persecution if one wishes to go through the activation process. Fortunately, the seeker is given the strength and comfort that he or she needs in adequate doses to keep the faith and see the quest through to its ultimate, inevitable victory, which will go to the truth and the light. The universe exists and expands because the truth and the light usually win out. This needs to happen here on earth; everything is on the line. The more enlightened people there are, the more likely the global transformation process will be experienced as pleasant and relatively pain-free.

The beginning of the SCAP is quite easy. It consists of deciding to go through the process. This is what is required to begin the process. It is remarkably similar to what evangelical Christians would call being born again, but we prefer the idea of letting go of the old ways of thinking to make way for new inspirations. It really starts by being ready for a flood of knowledge, insight, and love from unseen benevolent spirit beings who are ready and willing to assist us in this process. Spirit beings are located throughout the galaxy. They are generally benevolent and have advanced knowledge and understanding that will be very useful for humanity. This is the personal transformation that must occur in a threshold number of people to help bring about the global transformation.

The spiritual consciousness activation process is best understood as the awakening of the galactic human. This is actually a reawakening or reactivation of dormant human powers and levels of understanding that have been lost because of an excessive preoccupation with matter and the physical world. These abilities include intuition, empathy, cross-species communication, and telepathy. There are powerful forces at work to prevent people from experiencing these activation processes for themselves as such forces seek to forestall the coming changes. They will not succeed, however, because the new millennium and the Movement from the Source have come to usher in a new age of spirit, and the PAP and SCAP will help get us there.

The character trait of courageousness comes in at this point. Nearly every spiritual seeker has experienced persecution or ridicule for their beliefs. Spiritual leaders from many different generations and eras have experienced persecution from the authorities. The difficulty is that the degree of passion that the initiate generates is largely responsible for the success of his or her quest. Magic is really just focused intent, and the degree of power is determined by the passion of the dreamer. Don't be afraid to go wholeheartedly into the activation processes. It is the only way to know if they really work, for it is the way of the new world.

The process can best be understood as a continuous search for higher levels of understanding and awareness and the knowledge that one feeds off the other. The higher levels of understanding come from being aware, and awareness arises from understanding the magical, mysterious processes that are unfolding all around. It also requires that one release one's preconceived notions about what is really going on and be receptive to new insights and oneness with the Source of all that is. Hence, knowing to flow, and flowing, you'll know that both come into play here. Such is the wisdom of the Movement from the Source.

8

The Force that Animates the Natural World

The flow or movement from the Source is all around us if only we take the time to be in nature and appreciate the magic and beauty that surrounds us. This is of paramount importance. We don't need miracles to identify with the wonders of the Source because we can see the flow as it moves through the trees and the flowing streams, and the plants and flowers that bow in the breeze. These things can be felt at virtually any time of the day if we merely go outside and feel the breeze rubbing against us. That is the flow saying hello.

It is this type of spiritual reconnection to the wonder of nature that can still save us from the ravages of a military-industrial-technological complex that threatens to destroy the very foundation upon which all life depends. Whatever humanity does, it appears that some life will survive, but it doesn't take a geneticist to see that it will not be the higher forms of life that will survive humanity's poisoning and plundering of the earth. The less complex beings, lower on the evolutionary scale, like insects have a much better chance of surviving a nuclear exchange than more complex organisms like humans. It is through the experience of our oneness with all that we will find the answers that we seek and figure out how to live in peace and harmony with each other and with the planet.

The Movement from the Source is at heart a movement of spirit. It seeks to bring people together with each other, with Lady Gaia, and with all her creatures and progeny. It must be understood that the Source is a female vibration that will be and is emerging with her primary principles being to love and to allow. For this reason and many others, we strongly believe that this movement should be led by women. They are the givers of life, and they have a better-developed corpus callosum area of the brain, which connects the two hemispheres.

The movement refers to the movement of people toward the light and away from the darkness of ignorance, prejudice, and lies. It also takes a back-to-nature approach to living and worshipping. It seeks to help people understand that the same force that runs through and animates all of nature also keeps us alive and functioning, and that we must shift our being and our society to be in harmony with that force, or else we may well find ourselves without a home.

This is the understanding that comes with great urgency as we are involved in a rapidly escalating campaign to destroy our home in the name of progress. Climate change has become an existential threat to human civilization. Earth is a closed system that will find its balance with or without humans.

Once the understanding of the oneness of all becomes apparent, it will become progressively more difficult for the forces of greed and materialism to continue to pillage and plunder the planet for profit. We should be embarking on a plan of ever more elaborate celebrations to usher in the new understanding and the higher level of knowing that comes from being one with the Source.

A Giant Party

The movement is meant to be a joyous and happy process, a giant party to usher in the new age of peace and celebrate the end of war. This should go on throughout the 2020s, and the gatherings should include movement, music, and dance, as well as performance art of all varieties. People have an innate desire to be creative and to express their thoughts and feelings. This should be encouraged, rewarded, and celebrated. Movement can be understood quite literally as a swinging, grooving, dancing, undulating energy flow that is present with nearly every ecstatic human activity. It is the mass expression of these feelings and the outpouring of euphoria and elation that we desperately need to counteract the fear and anger that is omnipresent in the world today.

The beauty, wonder, and power of the natural world is often lost on us as we go about in our highly segmented and artificial realities. It doesn't take much time or effort to take a few minutes each day to get out in a natural place and feel the movement from the Source as it flows through nature and replenishes and rejuvenates the natural world. In this time, one can feel and experience that rejuvenation for oneself and thereby strengthen one's feeling of connection to the Source of all that is. This is a simple and healthy way to maintain and strengthen one's connection to and understanding of the Source. Springtime is a particularly appropriate time to experience the flow as the flowering trees and plants spring forth with beauty and color.

Life Is a Joyous, Cosmic Dance: All Is in Motion

The same Source that is within us animates all of nature and permeates all living things. This concept must be grasped as an essential building block to a belief structure that understands intuitively that we are all connected and that we came from and will return to the same Source. Furthermore, our overarching task for this incarnation is to restore and cultivate the flow or MFTS, and this includes being able to learn from nature and to appreciate and understand the beauty, symmetry, and exquisite balance among diversity and complexity that comes naturally to the non-human world. The way to truly appreciate what is happening is to see the connections between everything. We live in a holographic universe that operates according to certain key principles.

It must be understood that there is a physiological activation process that one must go through in order to maximize the flow from the Source. This process will be accelerated by the awakening happenings that are being planned to welcome in the Source energies that are flowing over the planet with the coming of the photon belt. These happenings may occur in conjunction with musical events and festivals where the attending crowds will be receptive to our message.

It must also be understood that we are all part of the same macro-organism, our beloved earth, Gaia, a conscious being. We are already late in meeting our task of being good stewards of the planet. Our record as the dominant species here on earth is abysmal. It will take nothing short of a global spiritual revival for humanity to wake up in time to the task that we are so egregiously neglecting, namely, steering our planet on a sustainable course into 2020 and beyond.

We are dealing with an ever increasing number of storms, currently manifesting as floods and tornadoes, largely the result of human activity. Climate change is causing dramatic shifts in our world and must be reckoned with if we are to have a long-term future on earth. Recently, the nation of Australia was ravaged by wildfires. This is particularly problematic as many species are found only on the isolated island continent, and hence we could be in the midst of a major species extinction event. The need for humanity to take a quantum leap forward has never been clearer or more urgent.

The spirituality behind the Movement from the Source is one of cooperation through understanding our intimate connection to all that is. This will result in a magnificent expansion of our sense of intuitive knowing, as well as direct contact with extradimensional beings who are ready and waiting to help us through this transition time. One of the central points of this book/project is that we are on the cusp of disclosure and nearing the integration of Earth into the Galactic Federation. This helps explain the abundance of UFO sightings and the movement toward disclosure that is well under way. It defies all logic to presume that we are alone in the universe. It is imperative that we gain a greater understanding of our relationship to the cosmos and the beings that inhabit it.

The key thought pattern that must be understood by a threshold number of earth humans is that we are ever-evolving beings who are on the verge of a quantum leap forward both individually and as a species. It is this latter aspect that is of particular importance to us as we enter the third decade of the twenty-first century as this is the essence of the global transformation. The political implication of this new spiritual understanding is that we must unite as a planet in order to join the spiritual hierarchy and ascend to a higher level of collective consciousness.

The plan involves holding constitutional conventions on each continent and then bringing those ideas together in a World Constitutional Convention that should be held prior to year 2030. The World Constitution and Parliament Association has created a viable blueprint for a new world government. Our situation is complex even without the threat of nuclear weapons. The issues of resource use, climate change, hunger, poverty, and air and water pollution all present major challenges that require a coordinated global response. This is where we should be putting our collective brainpower and resources.

The Choice before Us

The choice is now before us. It is one of a world where we are destroyed by our hatred, our arrogance, and our greed, or it is one of spiritual enlightenment with cooperation and understanding felt the world over. We are coming to the time of separation. This can be viewed from a scientific perspective, like distillation or evaporation. The separation refers to people of different vibrational frequencies separating in a process similar to mitosis. Humanity must now move forward to put an end to the old hatreds and divisions that have held us back on our advance toward co-creator status.

The Movement from the Source (MFTS) is, like the Baha'i tradition that came before it, an attempt to unite the various diverse and eclectic spiritual and religious traditions and movements into one overarching spiritual movement. This movement could include adherents from the mainstream monotheistic traditions and the earth-based polytheistic tradition. It could even include those who are currently agnostic or atheistic as the MFTS refers to a literal movement of water and air through the atmosphere and people. The times we live in require us to be open-minded about the present and the future. Clinging to outdated belief systems and ideologies will not serve us well moving forward.

Looking out the window from the room where I am writing this, I see several trees blowing in the gentle breeze. This simple exercise serves to reassure that the Source is indeed all around, that if we look we are sure to find it, and that she will provide all we need if we are willing to surrender to her purposes and go with the flow to the common destiny of oneness and harmony with all that is.

It must also be understood that we are not really disconnected from the same Source that flows through nature. There is one Source that flows through the natural world, that moves through our bodies, minds, and spirits with the physiological and spiritual activation processes, and that is uniting various movements worldwide toward the global transformation. As within, so without, and so it is with the ways of the Source. As more and more people undergo the activation processes, the world will become more and more attuned to the higher purpose of existence.

We are suggesting that all the old spiritual and religious traditions of the world be melded into a new spirituality that puts the survival of the species and the protection of our ecosphere at the top of the list of priorities for our global society. We must not allow old-fashioned religious ideas and beliefs to stop us from seeing the new realities of our situation. They will not serve us well as we move into meeting the challenges we now face. We must understand where we are and where we need to be, and we must make a rational, scientifically based plan to get there.

To summarize, we stand on the edge of the transformation of humanity and of human society. Either we will make dramatic and sweeping changes to ourselves and our society or we will cease to exist. We have poured so many of our resources into creating and improving weapons of mass destruction that their use would most likely destroy us all. This is a very real concern as the United States and other nuclear nations have refused to adopt a "no first use" policy. This must be changed if we are to have a future on this planet.

Furthermore, our economic system is run by corporations that exist to turn every living thing into dead green money. We must make fundamental and dramatic changes to this as well if we are to survive and thrive or this spectacular planet. We are badly in need of brave souls who are willing to follow the promptings of spirit and to heed the clarion call for personal and global transformation. We are literally on the precipice of both a potential nuclear war and catastrophic climate change. Whether we will rise to this challenge is the question of our time. Our actions in this regard will determine whether we will have a future at all.

Intermission

This is a time of reflection and introspection for those who are reading *Jewel in the Wake*.

It should be understood by all who are reading these words that this is a multidimensional guidebook; that is, the ideas and concepts expressed herein have meanings to several levels of existence. These levels include the personal, the national, the global, the intergalactic, the emotional, the mental, the spiritual, and the physical.

Without further ado, we present the second half of *Jewel in the Wake*: the millennium guide to the global transformation.

PART III

Earth Wars: The Trilogy

9

Welcome to Earth Wars

arth Wars is an idea, a concept, for a series of books and movies about a parallel universe remarkably similar to our own. The premise behind the Earth Wars trilogy is that we have arrived at the turning point in human history, and this is how we are meant to make the cosmic turn away from militarism and ecocide and toward a peaceful, harmonious world. Earth Wars is affiliated with both the Save the World Foundation and the Movement from the Source. We look to the zeitgeist movement and the Venus Project for ideas about how our society can be restructured. The Save the World Foundation will be a spiritual/ educational foundation dedicated to saving the ecological systems that support higher forms of life.

Earth Wars refers to the battle to save the planet as a suitable habitat for the human species. It also involves a battle for control over people's lives, control over their basic freedoms like life, liberty, and the pursuit of happiness, and control over what goes into our own bodies. This battle is best symbolized by the persecution of the queen of the plant kingdom and Lady Gaia's greatest gift, cannabis hemp. The story behind the vilification and criminalization of this most valuable of plants exemplifies all that is wrong with the world today.

Unfortunately, the dark cloud of conspiracy still hangs over the plant and the planet. The corporate giants know that legal hemp would forever alter the economic landscape, and they will do everything in their power to keep it from becoming viable commodity. Fortunately, the tide is slowly turning on this issue. The economic landscape must be changed dramatically if we are to have a long-term future here on this planet. We currently have interconnected feedback loops of consumption and exploitation that are working against people and the planet. Our priorities are all wrong.

By 2020, the entire West Coast of the United States has legalized cannabis for recreational use. Canada's legalization should allow scientists to finally do the research that will show the amazing medicinal qualities of this gift from Gaia. According to Leafly, Canada legalized cannabis on October 17, 2018, ending many burdensome restrictions on research. The *Scientist* echoes this, stating that Canada could come to the fore on cannabis research due to its having become legal in October of 2018. Also, the warm climate of South America offers a fine production area for the hemp economy. Food, fuel, fiber, medicine, and the green economy will be powered by cannabis hemp.

The battle over cannabis hemp doesn't just involve the one-eighth of the economy connected to the medical-technological-insurance complex, it also involves 80 percent of the value of the stocks on Wall Street. Cannabis hemp can be used in the four major categories of the US economy: food, fuel, fiber (including building materials), and medicine. When you consider packaging, you can see what a major change that could bring about, all completely biodegradable. It would short-circuit the agribusiness concerns' attempts to mutate and then patent our basic foodstuffs. It offers a way out of the fossil fuel crisis and the potential disaster of the greenhouse effect. The battle over cannabis hemp is the battle for the future of earth. This one plant could so revitalize our economy that most materials that are currently polluting our global environment could be retired almost immediately.

The movement to legalize this most beneficial of plants is part of the larger struggle for peace, for social justice, against racism and sexism, and for the environment. The battle lines get clearer every day. On the one side are the polluters and merchants of death in the military, the giant pharmaceutical and media companies, and the alcohol and tobacco industries. On the other side are the environmentalists, the young, the persecuted, creative people, and all those concerned with maximizing personal freedoms. At stake is the survival of habitats and species that are threatened by industrialization and pollution.

The conspiracy has almost run its course. It will soon be revealed by the apocalypse, an unveiling of things not previously known. The power and the earth will finally be given back to the people, and thus will the prophecies be fulfilled.

The crucial events, thought forms that move between earth and high realms signaling that we are ready and the time has come, have already taken place, and the thought forms have already been sent out to the Universal Mind. All that is needed now is for people to look within, understand the changes that are going on, and tap into the wellspring of support from the Source. The quickening of humankind is at hand. This is an actual speeding up of the vibrational rates at the cellular and molecular levels that is occurring with both humanity and the earth. This is aided by one's conscious participation in the process.

These are indeed exciting times that we are living in. The need for change has never been greater, and the opportunities to bring it about are also unprecedented. There is a plan, but there are many variations within the plan. The process is most important, and it will go on and move us forward. Hence, Earth Wars seeks to help people have a better understanding of the nature of reality in an entertaining, fantasy world format. This trilogy will outline a plan to save the world's foundation and allow humans to continue to learn at the earth school for millennia to come.

10

CHAPTER

Earth Wars: The End of War

The end of war begins and ends with a giant party. On this occasion, the party is to celebrate the end of war in a "thought creates reality" sort of way. This aspect of the Earth Wars trilogy harkens back to the germination of this book/project. We must put an end to war, particularly nuclear war, or it will put an end to us. We do not like the war metaphor and seek to put an end to it with this project.

Looking backward, the year is 1980 and Ronald Reagan has just been elected president of the United States. The pivotal event for this project would turn out to be a horrendous one, the assassination of John Lennon. It was the evening of December 8, and the lead character of this film, Dean Emerson, is recording at the radio station WYSP in Philadelphia on this, the day after Pearl Harbor Day. Dean is recording a Doors block in memory of Jim Morrison, the band's legendary lead singer. It is as this block nears its crescendo that the announcer breaks in with a startling announcement: John Lennon has been shot.

This mysterious tape, preserving that transformative moment in time, would lead Dean on his forty sojourn to enlightenment and set the stage for the miracles that are yet to come. The next six months would see Dean receive a series of transmissions, insights, and visions that foretell of great changes ahead for humanity. Dean's initial attempts to communicate these insights were rebuffed with surprising force, causing Dean to continue his quest underground. When Dean finally emerged after sixteen years of study, the world had undergone many changes, but the central one, the threat of a global thermonuclear war, either by design, accident, or terrorism, still remained a distinct possibility.

The original visions that Dean had experienced included a giant party to celebrate the end of war and the dawning of the age of Aquarius. These insights had been somewhat facilitated by his accessing of heretofore hidden parts of the neocortex using consciousness-raising substances while experiencing a live production of the show *Hair*.

Flashing forward, on December 22, 2012, there was a rebirth party for the planet in honor of Barbara Marx Hubbard's eighty-fourth birthday. The new earth has been born. It beckons us to follow it into a green and peaceful future.

Dean had actually experienced the exhilaration and ecstasy of hundreds of thousands celebrating this momentous occasion. Included in ending war is ending the war on drugs, as that is the war that is most responsible for preventing the rise in the level of consciousness that is so badly needed at this time. It is also being used as a pretext to persecute those who would challenge the mixed-up values of our upside-down society.

We are infinite beings having a finite physical experience. We must avoid getting too attached to the transitory trappings of this lifetime and consider the big picture. This offers a clue as to how humanity could escape from the crucible of the problems of earth trauma, climate change, and a possible third world war. These things could be avoided or sidestepped if humanity were to be united behind a higher purpose, coming together to end war and usher in the new millennium with global peace and cooperation.

It is interesting to speculate whether Dean had chosen this role for himself or whether it was thrust upon him. The answer, as it is for all such dilemmas, is a little of both. There are several other ways of looking at the notion of calling and answering the call. One way is to consider that Dean was a being from the future sent back to tell humanity what is in store if we are bold enough to take the high road. The second way is to consider the conscious channel for higher intelligence, and the third is to consider that the experiences visited upon him during the 1980–81 period, including his brother's slow death from a brain tumor, imparted such lasting impressions on his developing psyche that the die was cast from the initial revelations. We all come here for a purpose; alter ego Dean's purpose is consciousness raising.

It should be noted, however, that Dean had always felt that it was his duty and destiny to play this role. There was a lingering feeling throughout childhood, strengthened and buttressed by the tragic and twisted yet ultimately transforming events of 1980–81, that he had a pivotal role to play in the evolution of human consciousness and the destiny of human civilization. The United States, too, went through a change of direction in 1980–81. We were coming out of the Vietnam and Watergate periods. Instead of moving away from militarism and lies, we doubled down on them. Dean's feeling and beliefs on this matter would often bring him into conflict with the powers that be, but never to the point that he seriously considered abandoning his quest or giving up on his calling.

This feeling of destiny and calling was reinforced when Dean found out that John Lennon had been assassinated by a mind-controlled patsy who was used to silence the person the authorities believed could help revive the peace movement. The Source moves in mysterious ways, and that tragedy has spawned *Jewel in the Wake*, just as the message and music of John Lennon live on in the hearts of millions. For Dean, this realization was the last straw that broke the proverbial camel's back and led to the decision that he must devote his efforts to exposing this murderous conspiracy and restore freedom and justice to this great land.

The Final Battle between Good and Evil

The main theme of the Earth Wars trilogy and the end of war is that there is a final battle already under way between the forces of good and evil. It seeks to help clarify the sides and the issues in this final battle, although it exists as an imaginary figment, an idea, a concept, at this time. It should be understood that the battle is an internal struggle as well. This is reflected by Dean's conflicted feeling toward his perceived role.

The end of war is a concept that Dean had envisioned during the pivotal time in 1980–81. He saw that the road that the United States was then embarking on could only lead to environmental catastrophe, as well as massive human suffering and a drastic curtailment of personal freedoms, if we were lucky enough to avoid a global thermonuclear war. Hence the idea of a worldwide happening for peace in order to keep alive the dreams and fervent wishes of Western civilization's must renowned dreamer of utopian dreams, John Lennon.

The documentary *Above Us Only Sky* points out that the song "Imagine" represents the template for a global peace movement. It broadly outlines the belief system for a new utopian spiritual, but not religious, peace movement. It also goes to the notion that thought creates reality, that you must conceive and believe something before you can achieve it. It calls on us to imagine a world at peace where war no longer exists, because there is nothing to fight about, no religion, no countries and no possessions.

The current system locks people into ideologies. People are expected to parrot the ideology of their economic superiors and bosses. There is very little room for dissent or people who see things differently. It needs to be understood that good and evil are part of the same larger whole. They are mirror reflections of each other, like light and shadows. "Right is wrong and vice versa" refers to this reality. Currently our world system is set to self-destruct. The political and economic systems must be fundamentally altered if we are to be around past the year 2100. We as a society are so quick to label someone or something as bad without first taking a look at who is doing the labeling. In most cases, it is the very corporate and governmental interests that are stealing our future and plundering the planet.

The battle can be expressed in many ways, but it is really part of the thesis, antithesis, synthesis process described by the German philosopher Georg Hegel. Unfortunately, there are elements within our society who have twisted the dialectic in order to seek control over as much of society as possible. Not content with mere material excess, this group seeks to control the hearts and minds of the people, to the point of crushing all major forms of dissent. This is part of the larger goal of world domination that these groups are pursuing. This whole plan emerged in the first few decades of this century, and the plot is now on the verge of succeeding.

The groups, corporations, and organizations that are working together to create a new world order are varied and secretive. At this time, any plan is better than no plan. We would suggest that the groups involved lay their cards on the proverbial table and let the people have a say regarding their future.

It should be clarified that Dean does not expect to survive in physical form to see these plans come to pass. Salvador Allende said, "These are my last words, and I am certain that my sacrifice will not be in vain. I am certain that, in the very least, it will be a moral lesson that will punish felony, cowardice, and treason." Furthermore, killing the messenger will only serve to increase the likelihood that the message gets out thanks to the martyr factor. Finally, victory or death are the only two acceptable outcomes. One can only hope that the victory of world peace is achieved before the defeat ending in personal or global death.

The Turning Point

All this has now changed with the publication of a guidebook called *Jewel in the Wake: The 20/20 Guide to the Global Transformation.* Although the Earth Wars trilogy has yet to be completed, it will be a look at how we ended war here on planet Earth. This 20/20 guidebook, published 39 years after the initial visions about how the world would be saved, will prove to be the catalyst to getting other people involved in bringing about lasting peace on earth.

John Lennon said, "War is over, if you want it," and Jim Morrison said, "We want the world, and we want it now." These two come together in death and rebirth on December 8, and hence it is on that fateful day, in 2022, that the plan will be enacted. These two gifted artists and musicians have enjoyed enduring popularity and radio airtime because both were able to access the chords of higher consciousness in their words and music and hence were used by the Source to get out the message of the movement in preparation for the Age of Aquaruis.

Lennon sang and spoke passionately about such topics as ending war, giving power to the people, and being aware of instant karma and mind games. No artist before or since has gotten such important metaphysical topics out to such a large audience. These works refer to the period after he left the Beatles. John Lennon found his peace of mind prior to his assassination. As he clearly stated in the lyrics to one of the songs on his final album, *Double Fantasy*: "It'll be, just like ... starting over."

Ironically, he was finding personal peace and a new creative spark just prior to being gunned down.

The Plan

The plan is to hold a series of simultaneous worldwide happenings to celebrate the coming of our galactic family as well as the end of war. This project should be recorded and make into a movie. Happenings can be traced back to the Human Be-In in San Francisco in January of 1967. The next big happening was in Monterey, followed by Woodstock. The phenomenon took a hit at Altamont, but the tradition was carried on by the Grateful Dead. Festivals can be found all over the nation, and they have a key role to play.

The End of War parties are merely an extension of John Lennon's "War is over, if you want it" campaign that he waged in the late 1960s and early 1970s. December 8 is also the day after Pearl Harbor, the day that will live in infamy and the event that led to the development of the atomic bomb and hence to the nuclear arms race. Hence it is fitting that this day marks the start of a new era of global peace and harmony and an end to the scourge of war for all time.

A couple of examples of this type of event include the music festivals Live Aid and Farm Aid, as well Bread and Puppets, Wormtown, and Burning Man. Festivals present the setting that is conducive to peak experiences. They can be considered activation accelerators. The difference in what is coming in the future is that the festivals of the future will be focused on saving the world foundation. The many global rallies for peace could also be seen as precursors. Currently, we are experiencing a major uptick in anti-war protests in response to rumblings of war between the US and Iran.

Lest we forget who the real enemy here is, it must be kept in the forefront of consciousness that the goal of those living during these turbulent, tumultuous times should be to save the world foundation for future generations. Hence the enemy is those people or institutions who would threaten the support systems upon which all forms of life depend for their physical survival. These threats come primarily from the military and the large corporations that are funded by the Pentagon to manufacture their weapons of death and bring about planetary genocide.

The horrible mis-allocation of resources, symbolized by the obscene Pentagon budgets and multiplying costs of prosecuting consensual crimes, affects every aspect of American life, and no institution escapes without being beholden to the ruling cabal that seeks to tighten its stranglehold on US political and economic life. Consensual crimes are those actions for which both sides are in agreement and to which they have given their consent. Cannabis possession is the most common, but possession of other drugs and prostitution fall into the same category.

The larger effect that the usurpers of power have on everyday life is to create an atmosphere of fear and mistrust. This leads to a diminished lifestyle for the people because our strength is sapped by the double burden of working twice or three times as hard as is necessary because of the wastefulness and greed of the conspirators and the added burden of always having to be on guard. This is a situation that cannot be tolerated for very long as every person has their breaking point.

The cabal has actually been seeking to cause psychic numbing through tabula rasa, a mind-control technique being used on our society at large in an attempt to get people to submit to ever more intrusive government. This is so people will not object as the elites hoard more and more of the society's resources and squander them on their foolish and ultimately genocidal pastimes.

The Second American Revolution

This situation calls for nothing short of a second American Revolution. Not a revolution of guns or violence, but rather a revolution of ideas and of lifestyle. The time has come to say that we will not cooperate with a government that seized power through murder and that denies us our basic human freedoms. Our current system is held together by violence and threats of violence. This is precarious because the violence threatened could lead directly to the end of human civilization. This is totally unacceptable. All actions between consenting adults should not be criminal, provided they do not harm the person or property of a nonconsenting other. Another way to say this is to declare that we should legalize nature. Any plant that grows from the ground, our mother, planet Earth, should be legal in its natural form.

Fortunately, one will soon be able to watch this scenario being played out on video and via other forms of media, so there is no need for action at this time. It would behoove all who wish to help to end war to make an effort to communicate this desire to at least four other people. This is symbolic of the four directions to which the message must go out to in order for the idea that we really can end war by envisioning a peaceful world to gain traction. This is consistent with the traditions of the Native peoples all over the world. It is this possible future that the Earth Wars trilogy seeks to birth into the public consciousness.

The *Zeitgeist* movie trilogy does a fine job of detailing the situation and pointing us in a new direction. A resource-based economy is a sustainable model that we can and should move toward. The Venus Project, spearheaded by Roxanne Meadows and the late Jacque Fresco, shows us the emerging technologies that can transform our physical environment. A resource-based economy considers the resources available in a given bioregion and on the earth and uses the scientific method to determine how to maximize the effectiveness, the use, and the preservation of these resources. We would be wise to move toward a sustainable, resource-based economy.

The movie *The End of War* will be a filming of the actual events that will help to get into the public consciousness the idea of ending war for our entrance into the galactic community. Thus the party and movie are largely one and the same as the movie will include some of the planning for the party, as well as highlights from the party itself. Rock and roll will be a prominent part of the event. Who will be asked to perform has yet be decided, but some music from deceased performers will undoubtedly be included.

The staging and filming of *The End of War* will mark a turning point in the direction of the Movement from the Source, as it may well do for the world as a whole. The world has yet to come together to celebrate its achievements or to solve the remaining serious problems that still haunt us all. The need to put this pressing information before the American people is quite urgent. Come and see the show. Earth has become the greatest show in the galaxy. That is a big reason for our burgeoning human population: souls want to witness an participate in this climactic era in human evolution.

The "thought creates reality" message of *The End of War* runs throughout the Earth Wars trilogy. This is a fundamental concept for one to understand and live by if one is to play a meaningful role in the transformation process. This is because our thoughts are far more powerful than most people realize, and they can make a positive, life-enhancing change. The positive message here is that the process of aligning one's belief system with the true nature of reality results in a merging with the larger forces of the universe. This has the effect of acting as a magnifier and enhancer of one's thoughts and actions on a scale unimaginable to those who are acting out of step with the larger purposes of the cosmic plan. This is what makes it all worthwhile, for all the work that is done to bring one closer to the Source is multiplied and added to and comes back to that person as blessings and bounty for millennia to come.

This is the big problem that must be resolved if we are to tackle the many other interrelated problems that currently threaten our species. War is really about control and domination as no person or government that does not seek to control others would start a war. War has become totally archaic, and most people born since the dropping of the atomic bomb instinctively realize this. This group includes an extraordinary number of ascended masters who have come to earth in physical form to help humanity through the transition. It is a good bet that many of them (you) would be attracted to *Jewel in the Wake* as like generally finds like.

We encourage all who are concerned with the future of humanity and with saving the world foundation to upload videos of the joyous process of global transformation unfolding. This has been happening, and we should recognize and appreciate the power that image, like a vision board, has in changing our consciousness and hence changing the world.

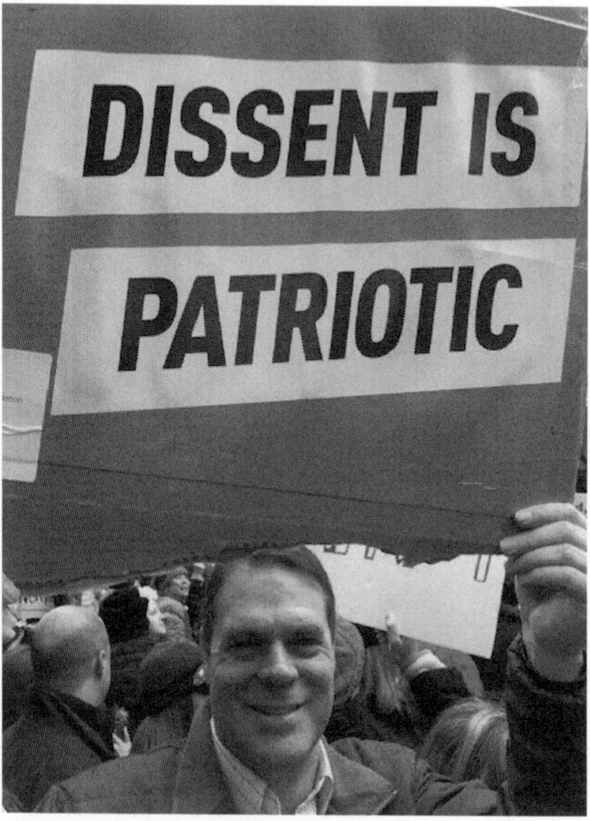
DISSENT IS
PATRIOTIC

11

Earth Wars: Reemergence of the Goddess

The second book/movie of the trilogy is called *Reemergence of the Goddess*. This movie will show various images of the Goddess reemerging throughout the plant and animal kingdoms. The images will be very sensual without being overtly sexual. The Goddess will rightly be the predominant spiritual archetype of the new millennium.

Reemergence will delve into a theoretical matriarchal society where decisions are made based on how they affect woman and children first as the life-givers and the future, respectively. It is also vital that we reestablish our connection with the Source of all that is, the Prime Creator, God/Goddess, through meaningful earth-based rituals. This is something that was understood by the Goddess-worshipping peoples of the ancient world, and that spirit of awe and reverence for the working of Mother Nature must be recaptured if we are to make it successfully through this transformation period.

Reemergence of the Goddess represents a conscious cosmic turn away from militarism, domination of the world, and excessive inequalities and toward a world of peace and harmony with nature and social justice for all. This can be accomplished if we adopt the edicts of love and allow these to be our guiding principles as these are the principles of the great earth goddess herself.

The new world will be led by women. We are recommending a group of five wise women to be the ultimate arbiters of the direction of human society. Their role will be to resolve disputes between nations and other groups peacefully and nonviolently. Women are more empathetic and intuitive, and less proven to adopt militarism and violence to resolve disputes. *Matriarchy* defined as a social unit governed by women or a group of women. We would be wise to give this a try, as Finland, considered the happiest country on Earth, is now governed primarily by women. This is an experiment worth trying.

The re-emergence of the goddess can be understood on many levels. It refers to the yin energy that is pouring over our planet and changing our values from domination, oppression, and intolerance to ones of nurturing and a renewed respect and reverence of nature. Inclusive in this shift is a deep understanding of the interconnectedness of all and the sacredness of all life. This requires one to be conscious of the ripple effects of one's own actions, and it beckons people to try to understand the great shift that is occurring on earth today.

The Goddess can be found in both males and females, but females represent the physical manifestation. Unfortunately, neither of the sexes is doing a particularly good job of demonstrating the qualities of unconditional love in a nonjudgmental manner, especially since the deaths of Mother Teresa and Princess Diana. It remains to be seen who will fill the void left by the departure of these two great souls, perhaps proponents of the new spirituality such as Marianne Williamson, Jean Houston, or Barbara Marciniak. Former Democratic presidential candidate Marianne Williamson is an example of a New Age guru venturing into the political arena.

The wisdom of the Goddess is intuitive and in tune with the rhythms, cycles, and flow of life. This spirit can be seen as a seemingly magical occurrence being made commonplace by the union of spirit and matter. This is how the earth's spirits can be communicated with and learned from. This helps people to develop a symbiotic relationship with the plant kingdom and the planet itself. Gardening is a good way to bring out and strengthen the connection between humans, the earth, and the plant kingdom. When gardening, don't forget to communicate with your plants and feel what they are relating back to you. Talking to your plants is a two-way street.

According the Candice Gankel Williams in the World Wildlife Fund's *Good Nature Travel* newsletter, plants move and do so with intention. A plant flowers and orients its leaves to follow the light. Plants also go to sleep and even play.

Wisdom of the Plant Kingdom Plan

An important aspect of this phenomenon is the wisdom of the plant kingdom. This includes how the flower opens its bud and secretes pollen or resin to attract the nearby bee or other hovering insect or bird. The plant kingdom has done this for thousands of years, and it waits patiently for us to understand its wisdom and learn to worship and respect the natural rhythms of life. This ties in directly to the mysterious and seductive working of psychoactive plants, particularly the female cannabis plant. In this context, the war on drugs is properly understood as just another example of violence against and persecution of the feminine energies.

The global transformation is predicated on the reemergence of the feminine yin nurturing aspects of the Source of all that is. It is a cosmic turn away from militarism, oppression, and destruction and toward interdependence, cooperation, and love. The feminine energies instinctively understand the sacredness of all life and understand it on a very elemental level. That energy must burst forth and reclaim its divine heritage if it is save the earth from those who would poison and plunder it for profit.

The plant kingdom offers us an omnipresent example of harmony and oneness with diversity. The systems that maintain various forms of vegetation can be compared to a Gaian mind, a maternal matrix that overlays the natural world and carries a wisdom far more profound than our own. There is much we could learn from this maternal matrix, and there are many ways that it can teach us. We need to lose the notion that our form of intelligence or understanding is any more profound than that of any other species. All of nature is imbued with divine intelligence. All living beings are sentient and somewhat aware.

Ultimately there must be a balance between the masculine and feminine energies on the earth and those throughout the cosmos. Yet the scales have been so far out of balance for so long that, like a pendulum, the feminine energies must be allowed to swing far in order to purify the earth and its people. This is particularly relevant to ending the threat of nuclear annihilation as nuclear weapons represent the ultimate example of male energies gone haywire. These phalluses of global death must be rendered impotent before we can truly experience oneness with the Goddess.

The ultimate example of the wisdom of the plant kingdom is the *Cannabis sativa* or hemp plant. This is the persecuted plant that marijuana comes from, its psychoactive qualities being the resin that is secreted by the female cannabis plant in its attempt to achieve pollination. The resin that is secreted is what contains THC, the psychoactive ingredient in cannabis. THC makes a direct connection between the female attraction of a plant and the receptors in the human brain. Make note that only the female cannabis plant secretes this THC-filled resin and that the resin becomes more powerful and more intense if it is not pollinated by another plant or flying insect. Finally, the act of adding fire transforms the buds into smoke (spirit) and ash, remnants of physicality. The THC or psychoactive qualities are found exclusively in the female cannabis plant. Smoking cannabis, when done in a conscious manner, can be considered the ultimate sacred act.

The Ultimate Balance

The ultimate balance is one of respect for and understanding of both the masculine and feminine forces and a synthesis of the positive, life-affirming qualities of both. This can best be done by removing the taboos, fears, and ignorance that is preventing the full expression of the feminine sexual goddess energies. This entails removing the prohibitions against sex work and allowing women to use their bodies as they see fit, with or without financial compensation.

Experiencing female sexuality in all its beauty and complexity will be a priority in the new era. Women will be in charge in the new era, so gay men will be most valued as helpers, advisers, and confidants to women. All people should realize that we are all products of a sexual act and that the kundalini energy released from two committed higher beings truly is the most powerful force known to humankind.

This process can best be facilitated by bold, self-confident women who are comfortable with their bodies and who are not afraid to use their sacred feminine charms as a lure to bring about changes in attitudes and changes in policies among the nation's ruling elites. Women must be willing to use all their mental and physical gifts to help bring about this shift in human consciousness and human society. This was attempted during the Kennedy administration, and not only was the president killed largely as a result, but also the woman who sought to help him see the light was similarly killed, so be careful out there.

One of the most compelling examples showing that our society has turned the truth on its head in creating its upside-down value system is how the consensual crime of sex for money has been treated. As we all know, legend has it that prostitution is the world's oldest profession. It can also be argued that it is the most important profession when it comes to preventing a society from going off a militaristic and technological abyss. This is because the power of the uninhibited release that can occur when aided by an experienced mistress can help offset the negativity that has so poisoned modern industrial society. Our nuclear weapons posture can best be understood as a potentially tragic and misguided case of missile envy as Dr. Helen Caldicott has explained in her book by that name.

The legalization of adult-to-adult pleasure for pay would be a sure way to help release the tension and pent-up frustrations that so many people, especially men, feel in our high-tech, highstress society. This would also be a great boon to the economy, offering women a chance to cash in on their second-best asset, their minds being the first. The legalization of all consensual acts, including prostitution, would allow women to get a tangible financial benefit from their warmth, compassion, and empathy. Sex can best be understood as a sacred ritual that occasionally results in procreation. An enlightened society would put sexual activity at or near the top of the list of all sacred activities.

Ultimately, the male–female relationship is one of those on–off, light–dark, positive–negative polarities that must be dynamic but also in balance. This requires that the goddess energies team up with the spiritual rebel warrior male and that the two forces align to destroy the old ways involving destruction and lies. The multifaceted nature of the reemergence makes it necessary that one always be aware of the presence of the Goddess, for it is becoming more pronounced by the week. The #MeToo and Time's Up movements represent the early stages of this profound shift in human norms and behavior. They represent the early stages of a female-led movement to take power from the patriarchy and create a new system based on caring, cooperation, and empathy.

It should be pointed out, for those who might have missed the connection, that the female human body is the closest thing that we have to the Goddess here on earth. The connections can be made on a number of levels. One obvious level is that it is the literal source of our being, the womb from which we all emerged at the start of this earth incarnation. Second, it is the undulating, pulsating movement of this manifestation of the Goddess that arouses, excites, and motivates the male energies to please and win over the female, to experience her love and support. It is this dynamic that has caused so many problems, especially the overlay of lies and guilt that the church and other institutions have burdened us with.

Reemergence of the Goddess will portray manifestations of the Goddess (read: women) speaking and acting out what it means to women to be physical representations of the Goddess with all the accompanying pleasures and pitfalls. It will require that women stand up and take responsibility not only for their inherent sexual and procreative power but also for educating men about the true nature of pleasure and togetherness. Women, many of whom already feel overwhelmed with work and caregiving responsibilities, will come to understand their pivotal role in bringing about a global transformation. This project is meant to be done by and for women, to empower them to discover their own latent power of co-creation with the Source, for they are the closest human representations we have to the Source of all that is. At this stage in human evolution, equality between the sexes requires that women take over at the highest levels in order to balance out male control of the planet for the past two-thousand-plus years.

The Dalai Lama has said that Western women will save the world, and it may well come to that. Barbara Marx Hubbard has identified a new phenomenon she calls re-genopause, where older, post-menopausal women devote themselves to dealing with and solving the larger societal issues that we face.

12

Earth Wars: Return to Camelot

The third book/movie of the Earth Wars trilogy is called *Return to Camelot*. This part will focus on the political and mythological aspects of the global transformation. Camelot refers to both the Arthurian legend and the brief period of the Kennedy administration here in the United States. This part of the trilogy will explain what must be done to restore peace, freedom, and justice to this great land by learning the lessons of our cultural and mythological heritage. It is in service to others and to future generations that one finds meaning and purpose in life.

> Camelot is a castle and court associated with the legendary King Arthur. Arguments about the location of the "real Camelot" have occurred since the fifteenth century and continue today in popular works and for tourism purposes. The Lancelot–Grail cycle depicts the city of Camelot standing along a river, surrounded by plains and forests

and a magnificent cathedral, the center for Arthur's Knights of the Round Table. The knights see a vision of the Holy Grail and swear to find it. Arthurian scholar Norris J. Lacey commented, "Camelot, located nowhere in particular, can be anywhere."

Camelot has occurred twice in our history. The first time was on the British Isles sometime around AD 1000. This was a period of wizardry and magic. It was also a chaotic and warlike time. There were tribes throughout the land who often resorted to force and violence to settle their petty disputes. It was the time of the Druids and the Celtic shamans, of sorcerers who could alter the forces of nature and noble knights who exemplified the ideals of honesty and chivalry.

The story has been immortalized by modern mythmakers like Disney and through countless books and stories. The essence of the story is that a boy pulls a mysterious sword from a stone and is crowned rightful king of England, but as we all know, the pen is mightier than the sword. This phrase, coined by English author Edward Bulwer-Lytton in 1839, indicates that communication, particularly written language, is a more effective tool than direct violence. The boy is crowned king, and he goes on to create a kingdom based on fairness, justice, and a relentless search for the truth or the Holy Grail. This search causes him to come in contact with forces and entities who have powers far beyond that of mere mortals, but the king and his knights have access to similar wellsprings of support, and hence a world of beauty and magic is born.

Camelot leads to the uniting of the various fiefdoms under the benevolent rule of good King Arthur. This leads to a flowering of high art and culture and marks a new era for the British Isles, leading to the greatest empire the world has ever seen. Indeed, the United States is the crown jewel of that empire. The Round Table is a symbol of these ideals as its shape implies a shift from hierarchy and division to a society based on equality and inclusion.

The second period of Camelot was the period when John F. Kennedy was president of the United States. This period is widely considered to be the height of culture and good taste to have come out of Washington, DC, either before or since. The Kennedy administration represented a brief period of high culture here in the United States. The round table implies all those around it are given equal voices and respect. It is inclusive, not hierarchical. Modern US history would be very different if the Kennedy assassination had not taken place. He had turned on the military-industrial complex and the generals and had expressed a strong desire to get out of Vietnam and put the United States on a peaceful and sustainable course. This brief golden age was cut short by an assassin's bullet. This has proved to be a pivotal moment in US history as the perpetrators of this coup d'état have succeeded in covering it up for fifty-six years, until now. *Return to Camelot* will show how we can return to those days of excitement and hope by seeking out the truth and then living that truth.

This project was hinted at briefly in the series on NBC TV called *Dark Skies*. This refers to an alien intelligence that landed at Roswell a couple of years after the dropping of the first atomic bombs and struck a top secret deal with members of the US military and intelligence communities. This sordid arrangement resulted in the aliens slowly but surely gaining more and more power in top political circles, spilling over into the Kennedy assassination and cover-up that continues to this day. The main thing that the aliens and the government are in agreement on is the need for absolute secrecy, lest the people figure out what is really going on. It is widely believed that we are currently under quarantine here on Earth. Insiders say that Official First Contact(OFC) or Disclosures is most likely during the 2nd half of the year 2021.

It should be noted that there are many entities from throughout the galaxy that are here to assist humanity in making the next great leap in human evolution. Examples of these beings are the Pleiadians, the Arcturians, the Sirians, and the Andromedans. They are primarily here to aid humanity, and they use telepathy to help steer humanity toward a peaceful and sustainable future.

We will most likely never get the full truth about many aspects of the goings-on of this secretive group that has controlled and run our country for the past fifty-six years. They are skilled at covering up the truth and have made the pledge of secrecy a requirement if one wishes to work within one of the many branches of the US government. This is an important cause for our drift away from democracy and toward fascism. The political power and economic resources have slowly been shifted from the people to the corporations because we have the fox guarding the chicken coop. Our politicians have been bought and paid for by our large corporations, and this leaves nothing but the shell of a representative government, a system also archaic given modern communication technology.

According to the *Washington Post*, the military budget of the United States is set to grow to historic highs in 2020. Representative Ilhan Omar (D-Minn.) has pointed out that the US already spends more on defense than the next seven nations combined. This was also the finding of a report by the Peter G. Petersen Foundation. Overall military spending has already increased from $586 billion in 2015 to $716 billion in 2019, according to an article by Jeff Stein and Aaron Gregg.

It is no accident that Americans cannot seem to get enough of the Kennedy myth and mystique, for the Kennedys were the last divinely inspired leaders in US politics. Furthermore, the obvious conspiracy and cover-up surrounding both JFK's and Bobby Kennedy's murder point the way to the answers we seek regarding what went wrong here in the United States. The conspirators do have a knack for identifying those people who have the most potential for doing good in the world and then killing them or otherwise neutralizing them. For my part, I would not be able to continue with this project if I did not perceive of death as liberation from the spell of matter. I should add that any alleged suicides or drug overdoses on my part can rightly be considered the work of this evil group. People who publicly criticize US military spending often are silenced by violence or overzealous prosecution.

Can't Get There from Here

The factors that are keeping us from getting back to the garden have to do with both the stars and ourselves. Our sense is that it is timidity and a lack of will and direction that is preventing people from living the types of lives they want to live. People are also affected by a political and an economic system that is determined to defend the status quo no matter the cost. We must never give up, however, for such is the struggle of life.

Returning to Camelot requires that one suspend disbelief and descend into a world of horrendous weapons and sinister forces so evil that they would rather destroy whole civilizations than admit they have made a mistake. These are the same groups and forces that ejected us from Camelot in the first place, and they themselves are growing weary of carrying on the lies and cover-ups. These groups will probably give way voluntarily when they are confronted with the indisputable fact that their actions are directly threatening the world as a habitat for the human species. Thus it is the positive vision that should be focused on. There is nothing to fear.

The story centers on a round table upon which rests the magical mystery box, the computer. This box relays and transmits information and correspondence to all who are following the progress of the Movement from the Source and the unfolding of the life game Return to Camelot. Social media represents both connection and opportunity for coming together and organizing, but it can also be a forum for propaganda and hate. It must be used to help usher in a new age of peace and sustainable prosperity for all peoples.

Hence the Knights of the Round Table are transformed into the knights of the rectangular box, and the quest for the Holy Grail becomes the quest for truth and the transcendent experience that allows one to merge with all that is and, at long last, return to Camelot. The box offers clues through its shining, shimmering images that dance their own photon particle dance through cyberspace. These light beams may well help show the way into the new millennium.

The third book/movie of the trilogy is meant to be a case of art imitating life and vice versa in a *Wag the Dog* type of way. Some version of this scenario should be playing out somewhere on earth, but it is based on a parallel universe in the Pleiadian galaxy, which parallels contemporary Earth existence. Many civilizations have gone through something similar to what Earth is going through now. Dr. Lisa Galarneau on medium.com states, "A humanitarian intervention is underway on our planet, led by several ET's and an extra and interdimensional groups known as the Galactic Federation of Light."[1] It is the birth of a planetary civilization that is destined to merge with the other peoples and planets of the Galactic Federation.

This parallel world features a vicious band of conspirators who seized power by force and trickery and who continue to distort and conceal the truth in a blatant grab at money and power to gain control over other people and the planet.

---

[1] Lisa Galarneau, "A Summary of Galactic Federation of Light Messages," June 27, 2017, medium.com, accessed November 21, 2019, https://medium.com/we-are-not-alone-the-disclosure-lobby/a-summary-of-galactic-federation-of-light-messages-762b42025a0.

This situation has grown so onerous that the only recourse our main character has is to put out a series of writings that explain how right is wrong and vice versa and thereby open people's eyes to the horrible abominations that the government is committing in their name.

We must mention the great Illuminati event of the early twenty-first century, 9/11. As the *Zeitgeist* and *Loose Change* movies show clearly, this was an inside job. The actual perpetrators, as with the Kennedy assassination, may never be identified. Regardless, it is clear that this was perpetrated by the cabal to bring about the Patriot Act, the expansion of the NSA, and a series of wars in the Middle East and elsewhere. One can only hope that the 9/11 truth movement bears fruit and that the truth about that fateful day is finally revealed.

The Backdrop

The premise of the *Return to Camelot* book/movie is that we are at the end of a cycle of darkness and destruction that began with the dropping of the atom bomb, accelerated through the coup, conspiracy, and cover-up surrounding the Kennedy assassination, and reached its zenith with the election and inauguration of Ronald Reagan, cresting with the presidency of Donald Trump. The perpetrators will be exposed and replaced in the 2020 period as the forces of love and light sweep over the planet.

The sinister elements that have conspired to steal our government and our history have connections to several aspects of modern world history. First, the OSS, the forerunner to the CIA, made an assimilation agreement with German secret intelligence prior to the end of the World War II. It was known as Operation Paperclip. This resulted in the formation of the Central Intelligence Agency, authorized by the National Security Act of 1947.

This inauspicious beginning was clouded in secrecy as this was, after all, a spy agency, and the secrecy surrounding the Manhattan Project was now becoming official policy for many areas of the US government. This sinister band gathered information and power and were eventually was able to pull off the coup that resulted in the disastrous troika of Vietnam, the nuclear arms race, and the war on drugs. There is substantial evidence that President Kennedy opposed all three, and surely Martin Luther King Jr. and Bobby Kennedy did as well. This group has had a dramatic effect not only on US history but also on world history.

By way of example, here are nine beliefs about the Illuminati, the group believed by many to be manipulating world events behind then scenes.

1. Skull and Bones is an Illuminati JV team.
2. The Illuminati were behind the JFK assassination
3. They are conspiring to impose a new world order.
4. The US dollar bill contains Illuminati symbols.
5. The Starbucks logo also contains Illuminati symbols.
6. It runs the NSA.
7. Nearly all celebrities are members.
8. It manipulates the weather.
9. It created the Beatles.

The central theme of the *Return to Camelot* book/movie is that our true history and government have been stolen from us by a shadowy group affiliated with the Illuminati. David Icke calls them Rothschild Zionists. They seek to consolidate wealth and power into fewer and fewer hands. It will require a concerted effort on the part of caring, committed people to get this wealth and power back. The good news is that this group has been so successful at outflanking the enemy on the world stage that the United States holds the key to the next stage of world history. To put it another way, as the United States goes, so goes the world. The best way to help is the high way, that is, undergoing the activation processes so one can know for oneself how best to help facilitate the smooth and harmonious unfolding of the global transformation.

This movie will show the behind-the-scenes maneuvering of the movement as it seeks to challenge the status quo in a noninteractive, "thought creates reality" sort of way. We live in a holographic universe that flows on the currents of love and imagination. If you can conceive it, you can achieve it. This applies to our society as well.

Needless to say, entertainment projects of this magnitude require a considerable amount of capital. This is something that we are working on at the present time, but any help or assistance that you would like to lend would be most appreciated. The hurdle of adequate funding will not stop the planning from going forward, for when the curtain comes up, the role of change agent for human history could well be played by the person who is prepared and who is in the right place at the right time.

13 CHAPTER

The Never-Ending Story

The goal of the Earth Wars trilogy, as well as all the concepts in *Jewel in the Wake*, is to save the world as a suitable habitat for the human species so that humans may continue to go through the physiological and spiritual activation processes, that is, to feel the flow or movement from the Source. Our current economic and political systems represent the gravest dangers to the world foundation. The political system with over two hundred sovereign nations is an inherently unstable way to govern a planet. Humanity's challenges in the twenty-first century are global in nature and scope. We are coming to the realization that we are all on this spaceship together and we need to find global solutions to planetary issues. The economic system is run by corporations whose ultimate goal is to turn every living thing into dead green money. We can take comfort in the fact that we are not alone; there are powerful beings and forces willing and able to help. The catch is, we must ask.

Making this shift requires that we collectively resolve to save the world foundation for future generations and seek to raise our own level of consciousness and concomitantly that of the Universal Mind. We all contain the seed, the potential, to become galactic humans. The key component is that we wish to get involved in the conscious cocreation of the new world that is the global transformation. As the great Jimi Hendrix sang, in his cover of the Bob Dylan song, All Along the Watchtower, the hour is getting late.

We are involved in the never-ending story, the evolution of consciousness. This is something that will go on indefinitely as humans are just vessels through which higher consciousness flows for a period of time before it moves on to other creatures and galaxies. We do, however, have the unique opportunity to play the pivotal role in all of human history. We can be the generation that solved the riddle of war and helped save the world's foundation, or we can be the generation that failed to right the ship, that missed the wake-up call and self-destructed because of its greed, materialism, and inability to evolve to the next level of consciousness in time.

This message of peace and hope could, and perhaps should, have been disseminated sooner, but there have been entanglements that have delayed its release. These delays have served the purpose of helping to show the true nature of the negative forces that have taken hold of our society and are trying desperately to prevent the truth from getting out. Fortunately, this censorship of our true history can't continue for much longer as there are currently a multiplicity of ways for one to communicate with other people.

The secret to a project like this is to pull the old Tom Sawyer trick, to make others want to help in the quest to save the world. The internet and social media are the big game changers in the twenty-first century. Unfortunately, both can be used for ill as well as good. Each person will need to find and rely on their own truth detector. This is aided by the fact that the best way to facilitate the transformation process is to utilize the transforming agents of sex, drugs, and rock and roll. This is difficult to publicize because of the persecution of the first two and the corporate control of the third. We will figure out a way to overcome these obstacles.

As long as there is one person who continues to hold onto the dream of a free and peaceful world, there is still hope. Each great luminary of the movement who passes through the transition, be it Lennon, Leary, Allen Ginsberg, Nelson Mandela or Ram Dass, should inspire dozens of others to take up the struggle in his or her place. We will be employing techniques from *The Secret* and *The Law of Attraction*. Not only is it the right thing to do, but also it is entirely necessary if we are to get to our goal of a peaceful and harmonious world. Furthermore, it brings the benefits of moments of ecstatic rapture and cosmic understanding. That is a point we wish to stress: It is in following one's bliss that one is most likely to discover and succeed in what one has come here to earth to do. This is a universal law, like gravity and cause and effect, also known as karma.

The Larger Goal: To Have Fun

The larger goal is to make people realize that becoming enlightened truly is fun and rewarding. It is fulfilling to do something good for your planet and for those who are to come. This may be difficult for some to see at this time, but it will become apparent that saving the world from both destruction and tyranny is the greatest rush that anyone can experience. The moments of illumination when another revelation hits have to be experienced to be truly understood.

After the insights are digested and processed by the nervous system, there develops a certain necessity to share these revelatory experiences with others. We who are alive and relatively free are the ones who can and must have the PAP and SCAP experiences. It is our pleasure and our duty. This involves helping people to see and understand the larger drama that is unfolding on earth at this time. This gets us back to the reason for writing this guidebook, to help people understand and appreciate what a precious gift this life is and how we must not let it be snuffed out by the ignorant and selfdestructive acts of a few. Furthermore, we earth humans have a right to partake of the earth's bounty as we see fit, as long we are not destroying it in the process. This right must be respected if we are ever to experience true freedom.

The good news is that the activation processes are indeed fun and pleasurable to experience. They consist of having a connection with the pleasure centers and receptors in the brain that have motivated humanity for centuries. Mass activations can be seen at such places as where certain movement-oriented musical groups play and through other spontaneous and planned outpourings of creativity and energy release. We need mass activations done with conscious intent to move the process forward. The first law of thermodynamics points to the fact that it's easier to move something when it's already in motion, so let's get this party started. The time has come for this process to be fully understood by the participants so that they may become conscious participants in the activation process.

The answer to the larger question of what is really fun is, like beauty, based on the perception of the individual. In pondering what is generally considered adult fun in this country, I find that nearly all the activities have some connection to the goddess energies or the physiological activation process. This confirms my suspicion that the only thing that can really stop this message from spreading is excessive persecution, perhaps even death. Short of that, the power of the message and the experiences behind it should win over all but the most the most hardened skeptics and disbelievers.

Your mission, should you choose to accept it, is to resolve to become a galactic human. This is a being who is in direct contact with beings from other dimensions because such a being has undergone the conscious activation process and has opened up the conscious channel to higher forms of intelligence and knowing. Furthermore, a galactic human sees the big picture, the larger issues, and acts from that higher perspective. Such a person understands that we are all one and that the law of karma is immutable and irrefutable.

The key to having fun in the context of aiding the global transformation lies in letting go, that is, allowing the transforming powers of spirit flow over and through one's being to sweep away fear and limitation. Yet, as the goal is to become cocreators ourselves, there is a fine line between letting go and giving up. The cabal would prefer people to give up on trying to change the world; they would have us leave it to the "experts." The challenge for the initiate is to learn to enjoy the unfolding panorama that is happening all around us during the 2020 time period.

Migration and immigration have become major issues in the both the United States and Europe, as well as in other places. One solution would involve recognizing that all humans are earth humans and, hence, citizens of earth. All people should be able to travel freely across the globe, given appropriate resource and economic concerns. This would be another benefit of establishing the new world government. Indeed, we should be welcoming to beings from other planets and galaxies.

World government would focus on the dual existential threats to humanity, nuclear weapons and climate change. All other systems, including the economy, would be run at a lower, regional level. The top priorities for a world government would be peace and ecological sustainability using scientific methods.

PART IV

Return to Camelot: The Life Game

14 CHAPTER

Setting the Stage

The time has come to begin the life game Return to Camelot. This could be considered the "what you can do" portion of this guidebook, a way for the reader to plug into this budding movement and help make its vision a reality. This game requires the players to pick a noble quest and then fulfill that quest. Before one can fulfill one's quest, however, one must slay the dragon.

The dragon exists on two levels. The dragon is a powerful symbol that ties into our ancient ancestors. The dragon also represents the lizard people and the reptilian brain. It exists on the personal level as one's own demons that are holding us back from achieving our true potential as humans. It also exists on the planetary level, and here the dragon is real yet intangible, a destructive force that seeks to turn all living things into dead green money. Slaying the dragon refers to understanding and accepting the truth of the situation and resolving to apply one's mental energy to making things better.

Return to Camelot refers to returning to the garden, a paradise where lush greenery abounds and where "Do what thou wilt" is the whole of the law. Camelot is a mythical place where all peoples live in harmony with each other and with nature. It can be understood as the Garden of Eden, that paradise before religion and guilt caused people to hide from each other and their higher selves. It also refers to the place where men are motivated by the highest and most valiant ideals, and women are pure and beautiful on the inside as well as physically.

This is largely an intellectual game that asks the participant to seek out the answers to the great questions of life and to seek to live the answers. There are three basic states of life: work, play, and sleep. Most adults achieve a somewhat equal balance of the three, with play being the catchall category. The life game can structure and give purpose to the play. It requires a ceaseless search for the truth and a fearless crusade for justice. This process is greatly facilitated by the growth of the internet, as well as the boon in desktop publishing and social media. The truth is what resonates with your core and your heart. The truth is about love and hope, not hate or despair. It is difficult, however, to find the information that one needs to get to the truth from the mass media.

Camelot is a place where women are respected, even revered, and where the feminine values of cooperation, love, and the sacredness of all life take center stage. It is a wondrous and glorious place where are people are cocreators with the Source. This is our future and our destiny. This guide is an attempt to birth these concepts from the future into our society and its most concerned and enlightened citizens. So come, return with us to Camelot.

The first thing that a person who wishes to participate must do is to look within and feel the connection to the Source of all that is. This can be done in a fleeting instant, but that connection must be maintained and strengthened throughout the game if the player is to be successful. Deep breathing and meditation are two time-honored, cost-free methods of connecting to Source and the universe as well as with ourselves. Spirituality is always with us, if we take a moment in stillness and silence to find it. This is the purpose of the activation processes, and each person must develop his or her own spiritual regimen to help foster and strengthen that connection. We are spirits having a human experience. If we can see the observer who sits beyond all we think we are, we can have a peak experience. There are many activation process videos currently available on the internet. Meditation is a time-honored way to raise one's level of consciousness.

The second thing is to decide what the nature of the quest will be. It should relate to righting a wrong in society. The game that we play can be called the Illusion of Separation game. We are all sparks of the divine Source, but our societal institutions create the illusion of separation. The player does not have to act in righting this wrong; he or she merely needs to think long and hard on the issue, to empathize with the people involved, and to come up with a theoretically workable solution to the existing wrong. It is helpful if the game player is able to document his or her insights and discoveries in such a manner as they may be understood by others who are playing the game or interested in such matters. The internet and social media are both very effective and accessible avenues to do this.

As the game progresses, the game players will gradually come together and pool their talents and brainpower to enact each other's plans in harmony and synchronicity. The game would be played separately with an online interconnected version to be, hopefully, rolled out later. The game is meant to come together like a patchwork quilt, bringing ideas and beliefs together to create entirely new and creative solutions to the problems that currently vex our species and our beleaguered home planet. This will become increasingly necessary as the current system's inability to resolve, or even effectively identify, the pressing issues of the day becomes ever more apparent. It is nearly inconceivable that we will be able to solve our problems under the current system of corporate capitalism and national sovereignty.

The game player is encouraged to think big. He or she should not put any limits on the type of solution that is arrived at, for we are entering an entirely new world, and we will bring with us the best of the old world. The enormity of the challenges before us requires big thinking. "What if?" should be the relevant query. Knowledge means no ledge, no limits. We should have far more technological resources and alternatives than are now available or even in existence today. Our technology is advancing at ever-increasing rates. Our possibilities are limited only by our imaginations and our vision of what life on this earth can be.

It should be understood that this game is meant to help develop plausible alternatives for the distribution and allocation of resources as it is eminently clear that our current system is falling apart. It will have to undergo fundamental changes and serious adjustments if it is to survive in all but the most skeletal of fashions. The isms of the past have been shown to be shortsighted and unsustainable. Our inequality has reached unacceptable and unsustainable levels.

The resource-based economy model is one to consider. A resource-based economy starts with an inventory of our available resources, done at a bio-regional level. Then scientific principles are used to allocate these resources efficiently. One practical solution is to use the internet to create a true democracy where people vote online about how society's resources should be allocated. This would be a true example of Democratic Socialism, the people deciding what their priorities are and what type of a nation and world we want to live in. This will require people to take an active role in creating the society they want for themselves, as well as for future generations.

Introduction to the Life Game Return to Camelot

Prior to birth, the soul goes through a stepping down of consciousness and vibrational levels in order to experience physicality. This process causes separation from direct contact with the Source, and this disconnect is exacerbated by familial and societal norms and pressures. This connection is further severed by the education system, which reduces every act to its component processes.

At some point, the entity has a breakthrough experience that causes him or her to seek to reconnect to the Source. The Source is our preferred term for God, the Prime Creator, the Source of All That Is. It should be a relationship that grows stronger through each lifetime. This prompts the quest that is the key to the Return to Camelot life game. Ultimately it is a quest for truth, driven by love for life and a desire to leave the world a better place for future generations. This is also pragmatic as we may well seek to reincarnate on this amazing planet.

The seeker will often now retreat into a fantasy world in order to avoid persecution and/or ridicule from the more mainstream segments of society. A fantasy world is an author-conceived world that involves magic or magical abilities, new technologies, and a historical or futuristic theme. Some may be a parallel worlds connected to earth via magical portals. This process may include tapping into transmissions from a higher intelligence of a higher-dimensional frequency. These entities impart the insight/vision of a giant worldwide celebration to celebrate the end of war and the joining of humanity in the galactic community. This is all good because thought precedes manifestation and spirit trumps matter. Our dreamers and creative people are our best hope. We need to encourage them so we can have many alternative futures from which to choose.

The life game should be understood as an attempt to have fun while seeking to enact the plan for the transformation of earth at this time. Fun is one of the primary purposes of our time here on earth. Fun opens us up to insights and feelings that otherwise can be very difficult to access. In some ways, this is the ultimate paradox, but a closer look reveals that this is the only way that this process can be facilitated. If it is not fun, then others will not seek to be involved, and hence it will be more difficult to enact the plan.

It will be fun. It will be the grand sequence of parties and celebrations to celebrate the coming of the golden age of the galactic human as well as the end of war. These will be held together by the game players, who will have their innovative solutions to the problems of our society. There will be plenty of enlightenment and illumination for all as the Source will flow freely at these events.

Lest one forget, in addition to ending war, we are also planning on eliminating weapons of mass destruction and legalizing all psychoactive plants. May the Source be with us.

15 CHAPTER

The Conspiracy Revealed

The coup d'état occurred on November 22, 1963. On that fateful day, the forces of darkness and repression that Dwight D. Eisenhower warned us about arranged to have President John F. Kennedy assassinated in a brazen power grab. On January 17, 1961, Eisenhower warned, "We must guard against the acquisition of unwarranted influence ... by the military-industrial complex." The reasons for this coup included the fact that Kennedy had promised to "dismantle the CIA and scatter the pieces to the wind," as reported in an April 25, 1966, story in the *New York Times*. He had also pledged to get us out of Vietnam and to tell the truth about our alien contacts. He had been disgusted with the CIA ever since the Bay of Pigs and the Cuban Missile Crisis. In an incredible coincidence, Aldous Huxley also passed through the transition on this fateful day.

The conspirators can be found in the CIA, the FBI, the NSA, the DEA, the Pentagon, and other alphabet soup governmental agencies. They are also the leaders of the large energy, chemical, media, and pharmaceutical companies. This was part of an organized effort to replace US democracy with creeping neofascism, and it has resulted in a society more polarized and militarized than ever before in our history. Unfortunately, this serves the purposes of the ruling elites and their evil collaborators.

There are groups that transcend national boundaries and governments who are pursuing their own agendas with some success. These groups include the Bilderberg group and the Illuminati, historically the Bavarian Illuminati, along with Freemasons, who are said to have been the group responsible for the French Revolution.

What really happened was that the malevolent interests that have been driving the nuclear arms race decided that President Kennedy was changing too fast, so they had him assassinated and have covered up the details of his assassination to this day. Furthermore, they have rewarded those who have aided them in keeping the truth hidden, not only about the coup and cover-up but also about the drug war lies and their ultimate plan to destroy the world if all peoples and nations don't acquiesce to their demands.

The Kennedy assassination was actually less of a coup and more a case of systems maintenance. This is because there exists a network of secret societies that have infiltrated and overtaken the levers of power of the political and economic systems of the nation and hence the world. These groups, mentioned earlier, have seen to it that wealth and privilege are concentrated in the hands of those who are with them, and they will act viciously and maliciously to keep out those who would seek to enact any changes.

This group has manipulated our history from behind the scenes, skillfully manipulating the media and public opinion so that the truth about what is really happening never gets beyond a committed few. The groups involved at different levels include the Tavistock Group, the Council on Foreign Relations, the Trilateral Commission, and the Bilderberg group, among many other secretive elitist groups working together to dominate the world and control people's minds. David Icke has called these people Rothschild Zionists as they largely control the world's money supply and use financial manipulation to orchestrate world events using a problem–reaction–solution process. He also refers to it as the Totalitarian Tiptoe.

David Icke is the author of over twenty books, and he has lectured in over twenty-five countries. He believes that an interdimensional race of reptilian beings called the Archons (or Annunaki) have hijacked the Earth and that a genetically modified human–archon hybrid race of shape-shifting reptilians have taken control. This group, also known as the Babylonian Brotherhood or the Illuminati, manipulate global events to keep humans in constant fear so the Archons can feed off the negative energy this creates. Icke claims they are propelling humanity toward an Orwellian fascist state, or new world order, a post truth era where freedom of speech is ended. Icke believes that the way this Archonic influence can be defeated is if people wake up to the truth and fill their hearts with love. This theory goes a long way toward explaining what is going on in the world today.

What makes these times so exciting, and so perilous, is that we are approaching the final stage in many end-time scenarios, from that depicted in the Bible, to that believed by the Maya and Hopi, to modern conspiracy theory. The Abrahamic faiths maintain a linear cosmology with end-time scenarios containing themes of transformation and redemption. Non-Abrahamic faiths tend to have more cyclical worldviews, with end-time eschatology's characterized by decay, redemption, and rebirth.

Also, the twin problems of climate change and nuclear war present an existential threat to human survival. These issues must be resolved in this century. Indeed, they must be addressed in the next few years or else we will be lucky to make it to 2030. As Jim Morrison sang, the time to hesitate is through. The call goes out to all who are awakened: This is why you incarnated. It is time to anchor the higher-truth vibrations here on this planet.

Cycles of Modern History

This conspiracy will be exposed because this cycle of history is coming to an end. The shock waves of the implications of the massive cover-up that has continued through ten presidential administrations will shake our political and economic systems to their very foundations. Concerned citizens should begin making preparations now for this epochal event. Regardless of one's beliefs, it is becoming clear that the earth is headed for some major upheavals. The specific nature of these upheavals is difficult to predict, but preparation and response-ability, the ability to respond, will be key factors in determining outcomes.

The reverberations from the shock waves should shape the secondary and peripheral institutions so that only those on the most solid foundations will survive. One way the world can come together and solve these issues is to follow the US model and have the regions of the world come together for a global constitutional convention. We would recommend that this convention be led and run by women and consist of a clear majority of women delegates.

The seemingly unending interest in things, ideas, and personalities from the brief Camelot period in US history is no accident. People, situations, and events that spark interest and even fascination well after they have occurred tend to be the most meaningful. Just this past year, we've celebrated the fiftieth anniversary of the moon landing and Woodstock, two transformative events. The people also sense that JFK was a man of destiny and that we were a nation destined for good fortune. While this may still be the case, the years that followed the Kennedy assassination saw the country embark on an ever more warlike course both at home and abroad. This course accelerated in the 1980s with the election of Ronald Reagan as president, which was followed shortly afterward by the release of the hostages in Iran on Inauguration Day.

These events are connected because the secretive group that took power with the killing of President Kennedy reached its zenith with the election and inauguration of President Reagan, a staunch Conservative who nonetheless poured nearly $300 billion per year into the biggest government pork barrel project of them all, the military and its corporate defense contractors.

This process has yet to be reversed in the United States. We spend over $700 billion on the military, we are still testing weapons in space, and we are still threatening to bomb those who try to cross us. This is no way to bring about a peaceful and harmonious world. We should immediately adopt a "no first use" policy with regard to nuclear weapons. We could start the global negotiations by getting all nuclear-armed nations to agree to a "no first use" policy. The importance of getting nuclear weapons under international control can't be overstated.

The 2020 period offers us a brief window of opportunity to challenge entrenched interests and entrenched ways of thinking and to sketch out a new plan for the United States and the world. This plan still has the United States as the global leader, but rather than lead through bullying and threats of force, we lead by putting the needs of the planet and people first and taking only as much as we need, not to fulfill corporate greed. This can be accomplished if we are willing to make an honest appraisal of where we have been and where we want to go as a nation. One thing we surely must do is move away from the policy of MAD, Mutually Assured Destruction.

Interestingly, the powers that be who are on the verge on enacting the new world order hatched their plan, along with creating the institutions to implement it, shortly after the turn of the last century. Given this information, we can thank them for not completely destroying the earth yet and tell them that their services are no longer needed. We can create a new world based on the principles of fairness, justice, and sustainability for the new millennium, if we are willing to leave the excesses of the past behind. This is a pivotal time and our last best chance for peace and freedom. An enlightened society would realize that we live on a spinning disc that has cycles and limits. It is imperative that we realign our society along the lines of sustainability. Indefinite growth is a recipe for disaster.

The process to unite the world politically can be undertaken by setting up regional constitutional conventions to pick delegates and platforms for the World Constitutional Convention. This should be a process led by women with the primary goal being to outlaw weapons of mass destruction and create the framework for peacefully resolving disputes between people and nations.

ICAN, the International Campaign to Abolish Nuclear Weapons, has created a workable model of outlawing nuclear weapons on a country-by-country and region-by-region basis. This process must be encouraged and expanded.

The Madness of Mutually Assured Destruction

This policy of mutually assured destruction (MAD) was developed because the pre-nuclear era thinking of domination and control over other peoples and the earth was brought into the era of nuclear weaponry. This potentially fatal flaw in human thinking has us poised on the brink of annihilation, if we are unwilling to face the folly of our distorted and genocidal ways of thinking. Another appropriate acronym is SAD, self-assured destruction. This is the unfortunate fate of a nation that could befall us if we unload our arsenal of nuclear weapons. Such destruction would be the result of nuclear winter, a particularly devastating form of climate change.

Then there's STUPID, the stupendous thermonuclear unpredictable population incineration device, which is what our nuclear weapons arsenal represents. We bring it home with STUPIDITY because, as we see with SAD, it's threatening you. Clearly it's difficult to contemplate this reality on a constant basis. Welcome to my world. Just remember, it's not just the current generations that would be affected but all the generations to come that won't get the chance to exist.

The MAD policy has never been repudiated, but this is not surprising as one constant of our political system is that no one is willing to take the blame for the really big mistakes. This is one of the most distressing aspects of the whole nuclear dilemma. Its mysteries are surrounded by the double secrecy of national security and concern about covering up toxic environmental mishaps. The doublespeak and flagrant pathetic phallic fantasies inherent in this bizarre and nearly genocidal struggle stagger the imagination. It is clear that a society run by women would not have gone down this road. It's time for women to take the reins.

When one sees and truly understands the oneness of all, one realizes that things like the murderous conspirators who took over our nation are merely a manifestation of forces within ourselves. This brings upon the realization that if one can reconnect with the Source that animates all of nature and created humanity, one can indeed rediscover the magic and mystery of existence and thereby help usher in the age of light, knowledge, and awareness that will be necessary to put an end to the ignorance, prejudice, and lies that have characterized this last dark cycle of human history.

Hence, while there may well be a murderous band of right-wing thugs who kill or imprison those who would disseminate the truth, we all have the capability of balancing the scales by allowing ourselves to be receptors to the flow of spirit and thereby agents of the global transformation. This is the purpose of *Jewel in the Wake*, to help others understand the stakes that we are playing for at this especially pivotal turning point of human history.

Life at this time may only be a game, but it is the most important game that any of us will ever play, for we are playing for stakes that are so cosmic and epochal in their proportions that we have no adequate terms to describe them. Yet the best game-playing strategy may well be to surrender and go with the flow. The important thing is to have an awareness of awareness—consciousness. If we are able to attain higher levels of consciousness and understanding, then we will have much better odds of making it through these tumultuous times.

The challenge, then, in the wake of these revelations is to help to build a world where people are rewarded for telling the truth, rather than persecuted and thrown in jail as happened to Julian Assange and Chelsea Manning. We need to enliven the public debate so that the media becomes a forum for new ideas and creative solutions to society's problems, rather than a source of disinformation and drivel. We also need to seek out the truth for ourselves. This involves understanding the higher truths and then determining how we can integrate these lessons into waking consciousness.

Courage Is Required

The degree to which these groups of men (and it has been men almost exclusively) have controlled and manipulated modern US history is really quite remarkable. They have seen to it that anyone who poses a serious threat to their evil plans will pay. Using Manchurian candidates and psycho-patsies, they have eliminated such formidable opposition figures as Martin Luther King Jr. Bobby Kennedy, and John Lennon.

Hence one who seeks to expose this murderous cabal does so at his or her own peril. Assassinations have historically been used to remove people from power or to prevent them from obtaining power. The criminal justice system has taken over most of the persecution going on today. I enter this role with my eyes open, although that was not the case when my personal persecution started. Regardless, to paraphrase a fellow Connecticut native, Nathan Hale, I say, "I regret that I have but one life to give for the movement."

Carrying on with the struggle requires courage on the part of the person who is heading down the road less traveled. There is always the threat of persecution, imprisonment, or ridicule. It must be understood that in a society as upside down as ours, this should be understood as a badge of honor. In most cases, persecution and ridicule mean that a person is helping to bring about transformative change in themselves and in others. This is that because people have a difficult time expressing gratitude and appreciation.

The good news is that the conspiracy has almost run its course, and the changing of the guard should be coming any day now. The stresses in our current system can be seen at many levels. Our technology has outpaced our wisdom, and our avarice is overcoming our altruism. Even if the system holds on a while longer, it will become progressively easier for inventive and creative people to get the information and contacts they need to proceed with their personal spiritual quests for enlightenment. This process can only help bring about the rise in the level of consciousness that will be the final arbiter of what happens to our species at the end of this cycle of history.

16 CHAPTER

Escape from Illusion

This is the aspect of the life game where the game player is required to face all those things in life that are held in such high esteem and high regard by the powers that be but that are actually of little real value. This includes formal education, material wealth, status, and social position. This is not to say that these are inherently negative things, but rather that our society has become so shallow and so materially oriented that we are missing out on the more profound and more sublime aspects of human existence. Our system is based on outdated and irrelevant criteria.

Escape from Illusion beckons the game player to confront those aspects of himself or herself that are preventing him or her from gaining understanding of the true nature of reality and of our planetary purpose. It rarely takes very long for one to identify those people and situations, and the demands on one's time, that work to prevent the activation processes. These demands tend to be the very activities that one is most engaged in at present, unless one has already consciously decided to engage in a spiritual or mystical quest or take a spiritual or mystical path.

The illusions of society will become all the more transparent now that the 2020 turning point is here. Then it will become all too apparent that the emperor wears no clothes, to borrow from Jack Herer. The illusions of wealth, status, and social standing will be exposed as a collective hallucination that is unrelated to what truly matters. The challenge, then, is for the individual to be able to discern what is truth and what is important for himself or herself. It is only in this manner that one will be able to keep up with the ever accelerating rate of change as we move through the 2020 period.

One obvious illusion that has recently become manifest is the nation that we needed to spend trillions of dollars to defend our nation against the former Soviet Union, now Russia. Our petty disagreements over our economic systems could and should have been solved in a much less expensive and much more humane manner. The Cold War was a long-running play that sapped our national strength and resources, nearly bankrupted us, and still threatens the world foundation.

This illusion was meant to be balanced by a glimpse at another type of reality afforded us through psychoactive plants and compounds. The link between nuclear weapons and psychedelic drugs goes back to 1943, the year the atom was first split and LSD was discovered. These two developments unfolded simultaneously until the forces of darkness and repression seized control in 1963. Today we are left with the haunting mushroom cloud as a reminder of the link and as a glimpse of way out, if we can only read the signs.

One thing that a society such as ours is quite good at is turning the idea of right and wrong on its head, and that is exactly what has happened with the splitting of the atom and the synthesis and discovery of mind-manifesting compounds. These substances, called among other things an Entheogen (God within) or psychedelics (mind manifestation), have been hailed by scientists and laypeople alike as revolutionary breakthrough tools for studying the workings of the human psyche.

Despite being touted as having done for psychiatry what the telescope had done for astronomy and the electron microscope had done for molecular biology, according to Maurice Mikkers in a 2015 issue of *Wired* magazine, these substances unfortunately were quickly taken off the market in the early 1970s by forces that did not want them being made available, even to highly trained researchers.

On the other hand, the splitting of the atom was accompanied by the greatest expenditure of brainpower and resources ever in US history. This has continued amid a shroud of secrecy and coercion that has brought all the world under a deadly nuclear umbrella. The splitting of the atom has resulted in an ever-growing military-intelligence-technological establishment that exists to consume ever more resources while revealing less and less about its true identity and where it is leading this nation and the world. The juxtaposition of these two issues and agendas, and the centrality of the Conservative Right, leads us to a better understanding of the forces at work in this dynamic interplay of visionary versus cop.

Our current president, Mr. Trump, seems to have no concept of or respect for the awesome destructive power of nuclear weapons. One can only hope that we will survive through these very dangerous times and come out the other side wiser and chastened, resolving never to let ourselves get so close to the brink of destruction again. As I write this, we have just come off a stand-off with Iran which included an assassination and a flurry of bombs on both sides.

The offshoot of the marriage of high-tech weaponry and extreme secrecy has produced sinister mind-control weapons that are used to target, harass, and silence opposition voices. The research and development of these weapons has been carried out under the auspices of the Star Wars missile defense system, financed the black budget of the CIA and other intelligence agencies. These projects continue unabated despite the end of the Cold War, confirming the notion that these weapons are really meant to silence dissenters here at home, in addition opponents to corporate fascism and exploitation abroad.

The Illusion of Peace through Nuclear Weapons

The illusion that nuclear weapons, military spending, or threats of force bring true peace and security must be dispelled once and for all. Dr. Helen Caldicott has identified nuclear weapons as the greatest threat faced by humanity today. This is the most dangerous illusion of all, and it is the bursting of this bubble of delusion and deception about what is in the best interests of the human race that is a central aspect of the Return to Camelot life game. We must choose life above all else. When in doubt, new young life should be given preference over those who are nearing the end of their days. This is another area where our society has its spending priorities backward. Also, diversity is preferable to sameness. This is a law of evolution as diverse cultures and ecosystems are more flexible and more adaptable when change is required.

The groups that have fostered and perpetuated this illusion are committed to the idea that they can maintain control over what is happening in the world, and if someone threatens that control, they must be eliminated by whatever level of force is necessary. Fortunately, our world has grown too small and interdependent for this type of thinking to prevail much longer. More-inclusive visions must prevail as we enter the new millennium. Cooperation and negotiation, instead of domination and military action, will be part of the shift.

While we're on this topic, we went through an interesting situation in 1998 with the United States, the United Nations, Iraq, and Saddam Hussein. The United States was poised to bomb Iraq to punish Saddam for allegedly refusing to let UN weapons inspectors into the so-called presidential sites. First we must overlook the hypocrisy of the United States, the nation that has always led the world in weapons of mass destruction since their creation, in insisting that other nations destroy their arsenals, which may or may not exist. The disappointment in Washington was almost palpable when UN secretary-general Kofi Annan returned from a last-ditch meeting with Saddam and announced that the two had reached a deal.

The UN Security Council then approved the agreement, but at the insistence of the United States they added the provision that if Iraq was perceived to have violated this new agreement, we would bomb them before diplomatic efforts were given another chance. This is what happened in 2003 with the disastrous Second Iraq War. According to the organization McClatchy DC, on October 12, 2012, some in the Bush administration had misgivings about Iraq policy. We will have to be dragged kicking and screaming into the new golden age unless there is a major change in the culture of fear and control that predominates in Washington to this day.

There are many illusions that need to be understood and then assimilated into one's larger cosmic worldview. These include the illusions of the five senses and the illusion of the material world, as the physical world is a particle dance of protons and electrons vibrating at different frequencies. Another dangerous illusion is the notion that we are helpless victims, alone and afraid in a world we didn't make. We can just as well be conscious cocreators, working in harmony with the higher spirit realm in confidence of our eternal, divine, true selves. As with everything else, the choice is up to us. Life, and the world, is what we make it.

Turning Point of History

Whether we choose to be aware of it or not, the next fifteen years promise to be the pivotal turning point of all of history. The crucial factor in how it will all come out is the variable of human consciousness. We strongly recommend that each person who has the opportunity to do so find the source of inspiration and excitement in their life and go with it until they are convinced it is time to stop. The biggest illusions are of separation, limitation, and lack.

It is up to each person which worldview they will allow to permeate their everyday thought life. The more people who become conscious co-creators with all that is, the more smoothly and harmoniously the global transformation will unfold. This is the choice and the challenge. Will we be able to raise our collective level of consciousness in time to avert global catastrophe? This could well be determined by you who are reading these words. It's up to all of us, so let's make the greatest save of all, saving the world foundation so future generations of human beings can do it all over again.

There is too much at stake to hold back at this time. If we fail to make the necessary changes in our world and to ourselves in time, then we may not have anything left to save. On a similar note, if we fail to stop the ongoing attempts to control nearly every aspect of our society and our minds by this evil cabal, then we must resign ourselves to the fact that we are living through the period in which human freedom will die. There is no avoiding our rendezvous with destiny. The threat posed by the Nazis was just a warm-up for the greater challenge that is to come, for the Nazis and Adolf Hitler were created and supported from the very beginning by the same groups and forces that currently hold the levers of power in the United States, and throughout much of the world.

17 CHAPTER

Paradise Awaits

The objective of the Return to Camelot life game is to get back to the garden, to return to that mythical place where people live in peace and harmony and conduct their affairs in the most upstanding and honorable way that they know how. Money is an energy that is meant to flow. If it stagnates, it causes many types of problems. The important thing for the game player to envision is what would constitute paradise for him or her. A significant aspect of the game is for people to contemplate how a personal paradise would look like to them and then to contemplate if their vision is in harmony with or pitted against the larger goals of the Movement from the Source and saving the world's foundation.

The obvious problems in our modern society are the extreme militarism, intolerant laws and attitudes, and a callous disregard for the needs of the poor and disadvantaged and of the planet itself. Hence, any paradise scenario worth its salt must make some provisions for dealing with these issues, at least in theory. This exercise involves contemplating how different our lives would be if money were not an issue. People are inclined to be productive and altruistic given the proper opportunities. This allows people to be much more creative and fulfilled. This scenario would imagine a world with no possessions and where people are motivated in their daily lives by something other than monetary remuneration.

The larger goal of this part of the life game is for the individual to identify for himself or herself what would make him or her happy. It doesn't matter whether the person feels that the goal is attainable, as things are going to start to change with startling rapidity. Furthermore, the goal should be focused on helping the person achieve a lifestyle that would make the player most happy and fulfilled during his or her remaining time here on earth. What would one do if making money was not a factor in the equation? We are stewards of resources for our time here on earth. No one ever really owns anything. We are given or allowed to use resources for the benefit of ourselves, our families, and society. Imagine no possessions; I wonder if you can.

This exercise is important for a number of reasons, but first and foremost is the realization that the best way to bring about a circumstance is to place the attainment of that goal at the forefront of one's consciousness. This is the time-tested way of bringing about a positive response from the universe, and it can't hurt humanity's evolution if more people will identify what really makes them happy and then seek to live that type of life.

The theory here is that once people experience the power and wonder of the activation processes associated with the Movement from the Source, they will seek it out more and more and thereby accelerate the level of human consciousness in time to avert the worst of the coming global catastrophes. Barbara Marx Hubbard has described the times we are living in as a planetary birth. She predicts that the people leading the way will be re-genopausal, postmenopausal women. This dovetails with the statement of the Dalai Lama that Western women will save the world.

Barbara Marx Hubbard writes in *Conscious Evolution: The 10 Keys to Saving Humanity and Healing the Planet*, "Into our hands has been given the power of co-destruction or co-creation." She then quotes Jonas Salk: "The most meaningful activity in which a human being can be engaged is one that is directly related to human evolution." An irreversible shift toward conscious evolution began in 1945 when the United States dropped atomic bombs on Hiroshima and Nagasaki. The response to this crisis has been an uprising of a new consciousness, almost a new kind of humanity. Since the 1960s, the metamorphosis has accelerated as millions of people have become aware of environmental degradation, social injustice, and the need for radical change.

The larger issue that we face upon pondering our collective and personal return to Camelot is what kind of world we want both for ourselves and for generations to come. This is not an easy question to answer, yet we are having it answered for us every day in the form of limited options due to pollution and environmental destruction. If we allow species and entire habitats and bioregions to go extinct or be destroyed, we greatly limit our options going forward. We need to create a positive vision of the future and birth it first in our minds, and next in word and action, and finally in the larger society. Again, it is at the thought level that the important decisions are made as everything proceeds from thought.

Where Is Paradise?

Paradise must be found within before it can be made manifest on the outside. This is why it is so important for people to experience joy and ecstasy for themselves, for it is those who experience such things who will show others the way through the pleasure portals to the wondrous rapture of the golden age. We recommend a fearless pursuit of pleasure in all its variety. Just do it, and just say now. The pursuit of pleasure is too important to be left to the officially sanctioned avenues.

The catch-22 of any large-scale enlightenment scenario is how one reaches a significant number of people without running afoul of the authorities. There is a seemingly unending number of ways that the powers that be, be they federal, state, county or corporate, can inhibit or indeed eradicate a movement based on expanding the level of consciousness in order to end war. The trick then is to find a way to work within the system so these authorities don't realize that this is really a plan to fundamentally alter the status quo before it's too late. There needs to be simultaneous movements to imagine and create the new society while resisting and breaking down the old. We need a new story as the old ways collapse in front of our eyes.

We had a brief glimpse of what a truly healthy, creative society would look like with the counterculture in San Francisco in the mid- to late 1960s. The summer of 1967 is known as the Summer of Love. It started with the Human

Be-In at Golden Gate Park. On January 14, 1967, about a hundred thousand people, mostly young, converged in San Francisco's Haight-Ashbury neighborhood. The Diggers established a free store and a free clinic where medical treatment was provided. Timothy Leary voiced his phrase, "Turn on, tune in, drop out." Unfortunately, the powers that be were all too eager to slam the door on that little experiment. That spirit of innocence and exuberance, of creativity and inspiration, must be recaptured in a number of places if we are to be able to return to paradise, to return to Camelot, to get back to the garden.

The flower children, a synonym for *hippies*, used flowers to symbolize ideals of universal peace and love. The term originated in H. G. Wells's book *The Time Machine*. Although the hippies were a natural and appropriate reaction to a society gone mad, there were nefarious and malicious elements within their midst who conspired to bring down the movement. Three prominent personages responsible for the decline of the flower power movement were Ronald Reagan, Charles Manson, and Louis Joylon West. Reagan was the California governor whose heavy-handed tactics used in crushing nonviolent resistance won him such favor with the controllers that they had him elected president. Manson was the charismatic perpetual con who was used to hasten the demise of the hippie movement by tarring it with the brush of bloody murder. Dr. L. J. West was a CIA mind-control researcher who worked with Reagan, Manson, and the cabal to break up any and all dissent and prepare people for ever greater forms of control by the powers that be.

Remember the Sixties

There are many positive aspects of the Haight-Ashbury experiment that can be emulated and duplicated in recapturing that glorious and all too brief period. The Grateful Dead managed to keep the spark alive through the seventies and eighties and into the nineties, and it seems to have been passed to groups such as Phish and to festivals such as Further. The Further bus is another example of how the sixties' exuberance for fun and cosmic revelation could be recaptured in the millennium period. This could be expanded to a traveling road show that brings the story of the global transformation in words, song, dance, music, and performance art to people across this great land.

Festivals such as SXSW in Austin, Texas; Coachella in India, California; Tortuga in Fort Lauderdale, Florida; Jazzfest in New Orleans; Boston Calling in Allston, Massachusetts; Bonnaroo in Manchester, Tennessee; Lollapalooza in Chicago, Illinois; Outside Lands in San Francisco; and Austin City Limits in Austin, Texas, show that the communal festival spirit is alive and thriving. This represents a powerfully hopeful sign.

The tricky thing here is that *utopia* literally means "no place," and that seems to be the answer to the question of which nation or culture one uses to model the paradise of the new world. This makes the co-creation task somewhat more difficult, but it also opens all kinds of possibilities and hence can make the process all the more exciting and inspirational as one creates a new world from the remnants of the old.

Our paradise is meant to be green, and it's meant to be at peace. We are searching for a land where the gardens are lush and full, where people live as closely in harmony with each other and with nature as is possible, and where diversity and creative expression are both highly prized and valued. We seek to be a group of creative galactic humans who wish to connect with and cultivate the Source within while living in harmonic resonance with all of creation. One can only hope that at least a good portion of creation will still be around when we finally do get back to the garden.

This is the challenge of escaping from illusion and building a new world, to take the best elements of the old and integrating these with the new elements that have been developed as a result of one's quest for enlightenment. Let's hope there is still time to do all this while preserving and protecting ourselves and our beloved planet.

The biggest obstacle preventing the rebirth of the spirit of the sixties is the crushing reality of modern life, the result of the nefarious behind-the-scenes workings of the secret government. We live under a debt-based monetary system where compliance is enforced by an ever-expanding police surveillance state. Escaping is virtually impossible. Finding a way to stay under the radar is a good strategy at this point. These secret societies and hidden agendas must be exposed if we are ever to achieve true freedom and realize true peace and harmony. The good faith effort put forth in the sixties was met with a campaign of murder and terror both here and abroad. This will require that we patch together the elements that make for such exciting and fun times in the past, that is, sex, drugs, and rock and roll.

The Journey Home, or Return to the Source

L ife consists of an intricate and elaborate learning process. While most people are lost in the spell of matter, there is a small yet growing group of people who will seek the truth and help humanity seek and ultimately find a better way. It is those people whom *Jewel in the Wake* is meant to reach. They can be found in all walks of life, but they are more likely to be on the periphery of society, trying to get by in a world that is not in synch with the higher vibrational frequencies that these people have accessed. To these chosen few—and many are self-selected—life becomes a constant quest to maintain and strengthen the flow or movement from the Source. These people realize that their power and their inspiration comes from a source both outside and within, and connection to that Source brings an awesome responsibility.

The journey home refers to cutting through the layers of societal conditioning and to understanding that we come into this life to learn certain spiritual lessons—and if we learn them adequately during this incarnation, we will be free to return home when we pass through the transition. We subscribe to the notion that earth humans are largely made with DNA from other planets and galaxies. Home is where one feels welcome, safe, and at ease or most comfortable. Spiritual growth is the goal of most Eastern spiritual traditions, and it is strongly hinted at in the Western ones as well. This life is an opportunity for the divine to experience the world through sense organs of one of its creations and for its creation to slowly piece together the puzzle and realize that the connection to the divine was never truly severed.

The point of all of this, however redundant it might seem, is for us to incarnate as form, having forgotten our true divine nature, and to go through lifetimes of diverse and interesting experiences. This leads to the eventual and inevitable conclusions that we are merely a reflection of a larger light, that we are holographic images of all of creation, and that it is our destiny to return to the Source that created all that is. Our other mission is to allow the divine energies and guidance to flow through us while we are in physical forms so that we can act as conscious cocreators of the new age of light and love.

Get in the Game

All life is but a game, a mirrored reflection of the light from the Source. Our job is to understand the underlying truths and paradoxes of oneness and duality, of light and shadows. Once we have anchored these truths to our consciousness, we can harmonize with the divine chorus that seeks to elevate humanity above the level of conscious beast to our true nature, that of cocreator with the Source.

Viewed from this perspective, death is not be feared but is to be understood as a reconnection to the creative wellspring from which we all came and to which we will return. The issue that we should be focusing on while physically incarnate is maximizing our connection to the Source energies so we may smoothly and effortlessly reconnect to the flow of spirit that drives the universe.

Indeed, a reexamination of the concept of death is of fundamental importance if we are to avoid a great misunderstanding. An appreciation that everything reflects everything else should help to raise the level of spiritual consciousness here on earth. Death is properly understood as the passing through a portal to another level of existence. The nature of the next level of existence depends largely on how well one performed in his or her previous incarnation in physical form. The only judging that goes on, on the other side is when we, through our higher selves, evaluate how well we did in fulfilling the spiritual goals that we helped choose in preparation for this just-ended incarnation.

The concept of death as liberation is not a new one to spiritual seekers. According to an article called "The Death Illusion" on LiberationUnleashed.com by Arya Nagarjuna and Thomas Metzinger, "The fixed belief in a division between life and death is a great misunderstanding. The appreciation that everything reflects everything else is the undoing of the belief in inherent separateness and along with it, conflict and fear." The larger point to be understood is that this life is a precious gift that we are given in order to learn spiritual lessons and to consciously evolve to higher levels of consciousness. If we keep this idea in the forefront of our consciousness, we will be more aware of the synchronicities as they unfold around us and hence better prepared to get on board when our ship comes in.

A Personal Note

On a personal note, the rest of my life will (hopefully) be an extended journey back to the Source. This is because my course is set on helping publicize the message of the Movement from the Source and related projects through whatever means are most appropriate and effective at reaching our target audience. The essence of the quest in Return to Camelot, the life game, is to understand the nature of the human experience. Love is the vibration of higher consciousness, and we must be in synch with the vibration of the universe if we are to tilt our reality toward peace and sustainability.

Here's hoping that we all have a good journey home and continue to go with the flow so that we will know what really matters in this upside-down, right-is-wrong world in which we live. It is reassuring that whatever happens here on this earthly plane, there are still many other levels of existence that are available for the enjoyment and learning pleasure of those who are ready to move on. This is the fact that offers peace and serenity to truth seekers in the midst of the most brutal forms of persecution and deprivation.

The journey home should be spontaneous and effortless, like Dorothy clicking together the heels of her ruby slippers and returning from Oz, so we must see through the carefully orchestrated illusions that have been masquerading as reality to the glorious paradise of the golden age. Just keep repeating to yourself, "There's no place like home, there's no place like home, there's no place like home." We'll all there get there eventually, so we may as well enjoy the ride—but what a long, strange trip it's been.

All of life flows from the same Source, and all living things will return to that essence in one form or another. If we can understand the goals and aims of the Source of all that is, then we should have a big advantage in helping to bring about the plan for global transformation during our brief stay in physical form here on earth. That should be at the heart of any spiritual quest during this pivotal transformation period.

The circle of life is really a spiral, an evolutionary spiral staircase, that is represented by the DNA double helix. The helixes match up at certain places along the spiral, and this helps explain the recurrence of certain themes and patterns in human history. The upshot of this will be a resolution of the underlying inconsistencies that continue to vex people who seek to put our society back on the right track. These match-up places parallel "right is wrong." We claim to care about children yet refuse to allocate the resources to care for them. We claim to want security, yet we threaten the environment with the very weapons we build to provide that security.

An important aspect of this whole process are the beneficial photon light energies that are pouring over the planet at this time as we move into position to receive massive direct activation from the galactic center. What this means is that as we move deeper through the transformation period, insights and understanding formerly available to only a select few will be available to an ever wider number of people who wish to attain cosmic consciousness. This is the understanding that must be encouraged if we are to make the shift smoothly and harmoniously.

The major components of the Movement from the Source include the physiological activation process (PAP), the flow of spirit through nature, the spiritual consciousness activation process (SCAP), it is the name for a spiritual movement for the new millennium. All these processes must be understood and activated in order for the movement to truly succeed.

One helpful concept people need to understand is that of the flick switch. This means that one can consciously, mentally flick a switch in one's minds to change one's perception of any given situation. Flick switch means that one need not be stuck in any given situation or thought pattern.

We've come a long way as a species. Still, our biggest tests and challenges are facing us right now. It would indeed be tragic if we do not make it through these challenging and tumultuous times. We are all here for a reason, and we owe it to our higher selves to know what that reason is. This will require that we navigate through the choppy, treacherous times that we are in currently and cocreate a global system that is both sustainable and equitable.

The challenge that we must face today is how to move past our dysfunctional system of sovereign nations and shift to a system that integrates the interconnectedness of all into its constitution and creates a means for solving problems on a global basis. This process is best done from within, and it is there that we must start.

It has already happened. Let the games begin.

May the Source be with you.

Glossary of Terms

consensual crimes. Activities between consenting adults that should be allowed but are currently prohibited by the government. These laws must be repealed or disregarded if we are ever to have true freedom in this land.

counterculture. A widespread movement in the United States in the 1960s and 1970s. It was both persecuted and appropriated by mainstream culture in the latter decades of the twentieth century.

dimension shift. This is currently occurring on both the personal and planetary levels. The pace of change continues to quicken as the earth prepares to jump to a higher level, bringing with it as many life-forms who are willing and able to ascend to higher levels of existence.

earth goddess / Lady Gaia. A sacred feminine being who brought us into the world and maintains our very existence from moment to moment.

Earth Wars. The book and movie trilogy that describe what is going on at this time in a galaxy that is very similar to ours but that exists at a higher dimensional frequency. The process begins and ends with a giant party to celebrate the end of war.

emerging galactic organism (EGO). The myriad interconnected set of changes that are creating the new world. These changes will result in a dimension shift here on earth, which will bring about an entirely new creation, the emerging galactic organism.

emerging planetary organism. This is the term for what Lady Gaia, the earth goddess, is becoming. This is a conscious macroorganic entity that encompasses all living organisms on planet Earth as its component parts.

End of War. The first movie of the Earth Wars trilogy, and the goal of this book/project.

flow. The felt manifestation of the physiological activation process, and hence the human experience of the movement from the Source.

God/Goddess. The ultimate force in the universe, the Supreme Being, the Prime Creator, the Source of all that is.

hemp for victory. The way people and the planet will win Earth Wars. Hemp can lead the way to a peaceful and prosperous world. It also refers to victory and peace in the war on drugs.

Holy Grail. This is featured in any Camelot scenario. The Holy Grail is symbolic of truth as well as of spiritual knowledge and understanding.

Jah. The Rastafarian god of cannabis hemp. Jah also refers to an ancient Hebrew term the Yahwehists use when referring to the true name of the Christened One. Jah is also the name of a spirit guide who helped write this book.

jewel in the wake. This refers to earth as a shining jewel in the wake of an awakened humanity.

LAST, TIP, SEE, LAY, EGO, BE. The six-step process for personal transformation. The acronyms signify the following, in order: Love, allow, surrender to the Source; trust in the universe; trust in the process; simply enjoy everything; laugh at yourself; emerging galactic organism; and be enlightened / be extraordinary.

life, liberty, and the pursuit of happiness. The immortal phrase from the Declaration of Independence, penned by Thomas Jefferson. These were the ideals upon which our nation was founded. It is up to us to make them mean something.

missing link. The agent that elevated humankind from the level of animal to self-conscious human. It is found in the psychoactive plants, specifically those that emerge without a seed or without ever being planted, the virgin organisms.

Movement from the Source. The Source refers to the Source of all that is, the God/Goddess. The movement can be seen throughout nature in the whistling breeze through the trees or in a running stream. It can also be witnessed and experienced in humans through spontaneous ecstatic dance and celebrations of all types.

new age, golden age, age of Aquarius. The period that we are on the threshold of entering. This will be an era of lasting peace and harmony between people and each other and people and the earth. Nations and corporations will no longer exist in their current state.

new world government. The democratic federal world government that will emerge from the wreckage of our current system. The means of implementation will be a binding World Constitutional Convention. This has been predicted by a myriad of seers.

nuclear arms race. A tragedy of epic proportions, regardless of whether another bomb ever goes off. This travesty against humanity and the planet must be ended as soon as possible, followed by the deactivation of all weapons of mass destruction. If not, we face a potential disaster of horrendous proportions.

parallel universe. This is really all there is, a now infinite number of ever-expanding parallel universes. To understand parallel universes is to understand the riddle of time. This parallel universe comes to us from a point well in the future, and its creatures bid us to join them.

photon belt. An astrological phenomenon. A massive influx of beneficial photon or light energy that is flowing over our planet during the transformation. This energy helps facilitate the physiological activation process.

Pleiadian masters or adepts. Disincarnate beings who have arrived near, on, or under the earth in order to help us during this time of transformation. They report to the Time Keepers and Game Makers who are responsible for setting up the Earth School and maintaining the Living Library.

physiological activation process. A reconnection of the earth human with the Source that created us and animates the natural world. This process is experienced as ripples and waves that run through the body and activate the pleasure centers.

reemergence of the goddess. The yin or feminine energies that are ascendant on earth. It also refers to the earth goddess Lady Gaia and all her magical processes and progeny that will show us the way. It is also the middle part of the Earth Wars trilogy.

Return to Camelot. The book/movie/game of the same name. Camelot is a mythical place where people live in peace and harmony with all of creation. This is also a process that the game player goes through while fulfilling his or her noble quest. Camelot exists in union with the Source.

resource-based economy. The intelligent and humane application of science and technology in providing for the needs of humans in the most efficient and effective manner possible. The idea was created by Jacque Fresco and Roxanne Meadows of the Venus Project

right is wrong and vice versa. This describes how our parallel world has completely inverted morality and hence is totally out of touch with the natural order of things and is headed for a catastrophic fall. This can be seen with the nuclear arms race and the war on drugs, as well as our too little, too late reaction to climate change.

war on drugs. The phony but all too real nightmare we are living through in the United States. The ruling cabal has declared war on plants, or organic compounds that grow from the earth and offer us a wide range of benefits. The main casualty of this war is the personal freedoms of the citizens of the United States. The plants themselves are more highly prized commercial commodities than they have ever been.

About the Author

A rthur Jay Berman, a.k.a. Jay-Arthur, is a shaman, mystic, and visionary. He has taken vision quests and undergone ordeals that have allowed him to access levels of consciousness and glimpses of the future heretofore unavailable to earth humans. He has tested most of the activation techniques discussed in *Jewel in the Wake* and beckons all who are so inclined to help in this great quest. He seeks to remain behind the scenes as the movement unfolds. This project is undertaken with the understanding that the threat to human civilization is all too real and that we need a new realistic vision and a new reality here on planet Earth.

The internet is the main source of material for *Jewel in the Wake*. Also, traditional books and magazines assisted in information collection. This guidebook is meant to assist humanity as we navigate through these very perilous and challenging times.

Contact Information

We'd love to hear what you think about the ideas expressed in this millennium guide. Also, if you would like and are able to help out in any way, we would be glad to hear from you.

Arthur Jay Berman

Our website: www.behappyhelpothers.com

Email: ajberman@comcast.net
1ness4all@comcast.net

Twitter: @JayBerma1, @Govern1World

Facebook: Arthur Berman

Thanks for reading, and we hope to see you at the big party.

May the Source be with you!